DELPHI

Monuments and Museum

By Professor Photios Petsas

Former Director
of Antiquities at Delphi

KRENE EDITIONS

Editor	Andreas Bagias
Translation	P-A. Mountjoy
Artistic adviser	
Plans and Maps	Dimos Svolopoulos
Photography	Makis Skiadaresis

©Copyright 1981 by «Krene» editions
16, Vassilis St., Theseion, Athens, Greece - Tel. 34.75.012

All rights reserved, including the right to translate or to reproduce this book or parts
thereof in any form

Colour plates	Reprotechnik O.E.
Typewriting	Photostichiothetiki Hellados
Printed in Greece	

The plans on pages 19 and 30 are based on those of G. Roux and J. Pouilloux

DELPHI

PREFACE

This new guide to the monuments and the Museum at Delphi is both a labour of love and a response to a specific need.

The need derives from the changes that have taken place recently in both the Museum and the site of Delphi. The Museum has been extended by the addition of one or two new rooms, and two or three others have been reorganized, while on the site a number of previously inaccessible areas have been cleaned and made accessible. And a number of new articles have appeared presenting new findings about the monuments and the exhibits. Because of all this, new plans of the Museum and the site have been drawn especially for this Guide, which also includes a plan of the Gymnasium and two of maps: one of the ancient world, and one of Phokis. This last helps the visitor to find his bearings in the area around Delphi, and furnishes information on a number of important sites that have been open to tourism in recent years thanks to the construction or improvement of roads leading to Parnassos and the Korykion cave; to Galaxidi on the West side end of the Corinthian Gulf; and to Kirrha, Antikyra and Medeon on the east side of the gulf. The world-wide influence and prestige enjoyed by the Delphic Oracle is also clear at a glance on the map of the ancient world.

This Guide is also a labour of love, however. My acquaintance with Delphi stretches back forty years – long enough for anyone to fall in love with a place, especially when that place is Delphi, which dazzles the mind and captures the heart at first sight. Is is now almost forty years since, as a young Curator of Antiquities, I willingly accepted the assignement request as Director to the then newly constituted Ephorate of Antiquities at Delphi – the first Director whose offices were in the Museum. Those were the years of Foreign Occupation. After the Italian Fascists came the Nazis; and then liberation. Delphi had survived yet another foe unscathed, as it had survived the Persians and the Gauls.

The first thing to which the visitor should turn in trying to come to an understanding of Delphi is the terrain itself, which is inextricably interwoven with its religion and art. In order to comprehend antiquities fully it is imperative that we attempt to shake off the burden of knowledge, preferences and prejudices that result from the current theories of modern times. As far as possible, that is. For it is not easy to rid ourselves of the idea that the world progresses and that we today are mature individuals while the ancients were but children. We have learned much from the passage of centuries, but that does not mean that we are wiser in all respects. Delphi has taught me the truth of that lesson, which I first learned from my mentor, Professor Konstantinos A. Romaios. It is for this reason that I love Delphi and that this Guide is a labour of love. Both the casual visitor to Delphi and the scholar will derive greater profit from their visit or their research, if they feel a true affection for the site and its monuments.

Ph. M. Petsas

THE SITE AND THE CULT OF APOLLO

The Site

A remote place, richly endowed by nature, Delphi became a sacred place from earliest antiquity, then a refuge for the mariners who eventually became its priests and, finally, a cross-roads and the navel (omphalos) of the earth.

Delphi was in ancient Phocis, but this does not correspond exactly to the district of present day Phocis, as considerable parts of the ancient Phocis now belong to the districts of Boeotia and Phthiotis. Ancient Phocis included about twenty settlements, of which Delphi was the most important, because the Sanctuary of Apollo was within its boundaries. The mountains of Phocis include the many summits of Parnassos in the centre (H.2459 m), the lower and flatter Kirphys in the south and their foothills. Among these mountains lie small plains, watered by the streams of the Rivers Kephissos and Pleistos (the ancient Phocians would have used the plains for winter quarters and the mountains for the summer). The gorge of the Pleistos is the main approach to Delphi from the Gulf of Corinth through the pass of present day Itea, which was Kirrha, the port of Delphi in antiquity. An approach from the east leads through the pass of Arachova from Thebes, Chaeronea and Levadia while a third approach comes down between the mountains of Parnassos and Gkiona through Amphissa. There are also roads from the west. Thus, when the sanctuary at Delphi attained importance it became a real cross-roads and was, therefore, called the navel of the earth.

The site, which lies at an altitude of 500-700 m, is dominated by the cliffs of the Phaidriades between which runs the Kastalian Spring, whose waters first gave Delphi its importance. The panoramic view from the site encompasses the sheer grey-green sides of Mt Kirphys, the gorge of the Pleistos running through the plain of Amphissa and Itea, the sea of ancient Kirrha and, beyond it, the Gulf of Corinth and the endless mountains of the Peloponnese. It is a marvellous view of great natural beauty, to which the vast silver-green olive groves have been added by man.

The Prehistory

In remotest antiquity the site was perhaps of only limited importance; as far as is known man was only present from the third millenium BC. The first settlement was on the coast in the bay of Kirrha (or Krisa) and lasted from the beginning of the Bronze Age down to Mycenaean times, but after 1600 BC a higher settlement further inland attained importance, near the present day Chryso, which is identified with Krisa of historical times. Higher still a small plain with an acropolis called Lycoreia near the Corycian Cave was also inhabited in the Bronze Age. In Mycenaean times, from at least 1400 BC, Delphi, the "rocky Pytho" of Homer, was the sanctuary of a female deity, Ge or Athena, who gave oracles through a prophetess. Other gods probably worshipped were Poseidon and Dionysus while, later, sacred rocks also received some kind of cult (the Omphalos, the Stone of Kronos), as did the hero Pyrrhos or Neoptolemos. Mycenaean Delphi was destroyed by a rock fall towards the end of the Bronze Age.

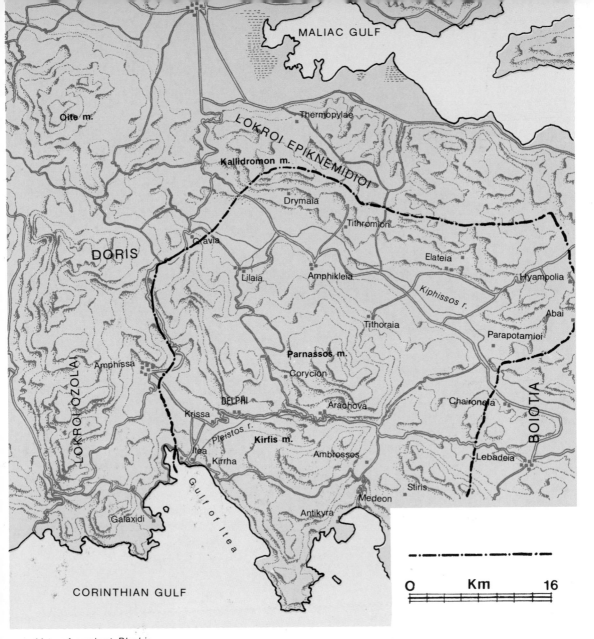

Map of ancient Phokis.

Early Historical Times

Delphi prospered again in the 8th century BC and the first information about the Apollo cult belongs to this period. In the first lines of the play "The Eumenides" by Aeschylus (458 BC) the Pythia relates that Ge, the mother of the gods and the first prophetess, was succeeded by her daughters, Themis and then the Titan, Phoebe, who gave her name to Phoebus Apollo. The complete myth, or a variation of it, is preserved in the so-called Homeric Hymn to Pythian Apollo (7th century BC). According to this Hymn Apollo built his first temple in a wooded grove at Delphi and became the first male possessor of the site, having killed the Pytho, a

General view of Delphi.

female serpent who guarded the prophetic spring of Kassotis. To purify himself of this crime Apollo went to the Vale of Tempe, from whence he brought the laurel with which he built the first temple. He gave oracles in the shrine of Ge (or Gaia) through a Pythia, who sat bound at the mouth of a chasm in the earth from which 'vapours' arose. The first priests of Apollo were Cretans from Knossos, whom Apollo, in the guise of a dolphin, drove to Kirrha after a wandering sea voyage. The mariners asked the god how they could survive in such a barren place and he replied that they would live effortlessly from the offerings of his worshippers. The Cretan priests introduced the worship of Apollo Delphinios (the Dolphin) to Delphi and brought with them a very old wooden idol (xoanon), which they perhaps changed the name of the Pytho to that of Delphi.

In the mid-8th century BC the brothers Trophonios and Agamedes, sons of Erginos, who were famous for other exploits, built the first ashlar masonry temple. The oracle gained a great reputation not only in Greece but through all the then known world. Greek cities and private citizens as well as foreign kings consulted it and offered rich gifts. There is a myth that Zeus, wishing to find the centre of the earth, freed an eagle at each end of the world and that they met at Delphi, which thus gained the reputation of the 'navel of the earth'; an omphalos (navel stone) became one of its holy emblems.

The wealth accumulated by Delphi aroused the envy of Kirrha (Krisa), who then taxed the visiting worshippers. This caused the F i r s t S a c r e d W a r (600-586BC) waged by the Amphictyonic League against Kirrha, which was destroyed in 590 BC.

The Amphictyonic League

This was composed of twelve tribes from Central Greece, Attica, Euboea and the north-east Peloponnese and had its centre initially at the shrine of Demeter at Anthele near Thermopylae; they were the Ainianes, Achaians, Phthiotians, Dolopes, Dorians, Thessalians, Ionians, Lokrians, Malians, Magnetes, Perrhaibians and Phocians. Their representatives, of which there were two per tribe called Ieromnemones, did not represent their cities but their tribes. If necessary, the so-called Pylagorai could be sent to Thermopylae and a general assembly could also be called which was open to all the citizens of the cities in the League. In the 7th century BC the League decided that Delphi should become its second centre and, after that, they met every spring (in the month of Bysios) at Anthele and every autumn (in the month of Boukatios) at Delphi. It was the fate of the sanctuary to be involved in three more Sacred Wars, making a total of four in 250 years. The priests of Apollo did not play a passive role in these events and, as the oracle was the hub of the Greek and foreign world, they had enormous influence.

The Amphictyonic League organised the Pythian Games and administered the sanctuary acting with the people of Delphi. The people probably had an oligarchic government as only the leaders had political rights. Every year probably nine prytaneis (rectors) were chosen, one of whom was the eponymous archon. A council of six members was chosen every six months and the ruling body was a popular assembly. The Delphians appointed the Pythia, the two priests of Apollo, two "prophets" and five "holy men". It collected the price for each oracle (pelanos), granted the privilege of promanteia (precedence in consulting the oracle) and saw to the general organisation.

The Oracle

The Oracle of Dodona was honoured as the oldest of the great panhellenic sanctuaries and Olympia was very well-known because of the Olympian Games, but no sanctuary surpassed Delphi in reputation and wealth, owing to its oracle and games. Although the ancient authors give much information about the oracle, many problems unfortunately still remain concerning its character and procedure.

Everything in Greece has a mythological origin. Parnassos, the eponymous hero of Mount Parnassos, was said to be the first to prophesy from bird flight: thus this kind of prophesy probably began in a place with much bird life. Another legend says that Delphos, the eponymous hero of Delphi, was the first to read entrails, while Amphictyon, the eponymous hero of the Amphictyonic League, was the first to interpret dreams. The so-called Pyrkooi prophesied from the flames of the sacred fire at Delphi. Elsewhere in Greece the pebbles used for prophesy were called Thriai, but at Delphi mythology says the Thriai were nymphs who actually prophesied. Myth and tradition show clearly that every method of prophesy, such as birds, entrails, dreams and pebbles, was known at Delphi.

The famous Delphic Oracle, however, owed its reputation equally to another form of prophesy: Apollo himself spoke through the Pythia. Originally the Oracle spoke only once a year, probably when Apollo's birthday was celebrated on the 7th day of Bysios (Feb-Mar). From the 6th century BC onwards, as patronage increased, the Oracle prophesied on the 7th day of every month, except for the three winter months when Apollo went to the Hyperboreans and left the sanctuary in the hands of Dionysos: thus, the calm god of light gave up his sanctuary to the god of wine and revelry, who had his own temple next to that of Apollo.

The Pythia was a woman over fifty who left her family to enter the service of Apollo and lived in a special dwelling in the sanctuary so that she should remain pure. She wore virgin white in spite of her age and followed certain holy precepts. It was not necessary that she be beautiful or of good family. Initially there was only one Pythia, but, as the reputation and patronage of the Oracle increased, two more were added. This was still not enough, so the privilege of promanteia can be readily appreciated. This was given by the Delphians to cities and private citizens along with other privileges such as proxenia (the official representation of a city) and asylia (immunity). Cities who had a Representative at Delphi could consult the Oracle on any day, if the god was willing. To ascertain this a goat was sacrificed but was first sprinkled with cold water; if it shivered, the god had no objection.

A suppliant first paid the pelanos and provided animals for the sacrifice and for the sacred table. He drew lot for order of preference. On the morning of the day of prophesy the Pythia would go to the Kastalian Spring at daybreak to purify herself. She would drink from the other sacred spring, Kassotis, and chew laurel. The priests, who had also washed in Kastalia, ceremoniously escorted the Pythia to the inner shrine (adyton) of the temple. The sacred tripod, the chair of Apollo, was supposed to be here and the Pythia would sit on it, thus taking the place of the god. The tripod was by the mouth of the chasm, the site of the omphalos, the grave of Dionysos and the gold statue of Apollo. The suppliant would also be ceremoniously escorted to the inner shrine and put in a special seat, without seeing the Pythia, who was separated by a curtain. Meanwhile the priests had prepared the sacrifice and lit the fire on the great altar (a gift from Chios). City representatives and private individuals assembled piously round the altar outside the temple and awaited their turn. First the Delphians consulted the Oracle, then those who had the privilege of promanteia and finally everyone else, in an order determined by lot.

The suppliants put their question, written or oral, through one of the priests who read it to the Pythia, who was out of sight and hypnotised from chewing laurel leaves, and from the incense and smoke. She replied in incoherent words and incomprehensible shouts which the priests interpreted into hexameters and the suppliant took this written answer with him. The answer, which was ambiguous, was interpreted by the suppliant as it pleased him and, only if the future turned out otherwise, did he see the true answer. This explains the epithet Loxian Apollo, the Oblique One. One of the most famous ambiguous oracles is the reply to Croesus, king of Lydia, who asked if he would defeat the Persians. The Oracle replied, 'If Croesus crosses the Halys, a great power will be destroyed'. Croesus interpreted the oracle in his favour, crossed the River Halys between Lydia and Persia with a great army and was defeated. The Oracle had been right again.

The Pythian Games

Originally these Games took place every eight years and consisted of musical contests with poetic hymns to Apollo accompanied by the lyre. After the First Sacred War the Amphictyonic League took over the management of the sanctuary and reorganised the Games, enriching them with new contests and arranging that they should be held every four years in the third year of the Olympiads in the month of Boukatios (end of August). The prizes were laurel crowns from the oldest laurel in the Vale of Tempe and the victors obtained the right to set up their statue in the sanctuary. A truce was announced three months beforehand all over Greece so that participants could assemble from the furthest parts and get home again. Each state sent a delegation who were named theoroi (watchers).

The festival lasted seven days. On the first day there was a sacrifice of three bulls followed by a sacred drama showing the slaughter of the serpent by Apollo. Plutarch mentions that this was called the Stepteria. On the second day a great procession took place in which the priests in their rich vestments, the delegations from the states, the competitors, etc. took part, all bearing gifts to the god. It set out from the Halos, a circular area in front of the Treasury of the Athenians. In front of the temple a huge sacrifice of a hundred bulls (a hecatomb) took place on the great altar from Chios. On the third day at a great banquet the sacrifices of the preceding day were ceremoniously eaten and the power of the god thus imbibed. On the fourth day drama contests were held in which hymns to Apollo were performed with the lyre or flute, either by a soloist or with a choir, and tragedies and comedies were put on. On the fifth day there were contests in the stadium. The dolichos (long distance race) was twelve courses of the stadium, the stadion was a race of one stade (178.35 m) while the diaulos was a race of two stades. The pentathlon consisted of five contests (running, wrestling, jumping, throwing the discus and the javelin) and there were also separate wrestling and boxing contests, a pankration, which was a combination of boxing and wrestling, and finally a race of men under arms. The Amphictyonic League introduced the chariot race with two and four horse chariots. These races occurred in the hippodrome on the sixth day while the gymnastic contests were on the seventh day and, as one day was often not sufficient, they took an extra day so that the contests lasted eight days in all. The Pythian Games differed from the other panhellenic games because they included contests with religious hymns accompanied by the lyre and flute. Music in a broader sense than that of today (ie. including the associated arts) was the especial love of Apollo.

The Reputation of the Oracle and the Treasuries

From the 8th century BC onwards and especially in the Archaic Period, the reputation of the Oracle spread through all the then known world and Greeks and foreigners consulted it, the Greeks especially before founding a colony, as Apollo was considered the archigetes (founder) of colonies; indeed there are many called Apollonia after him. Syracuse and Croton in Magna Craecia, Cyrene in Africa and Thasos in the north Aegean are some of the more important colonies who held Delphic Apollo as their protector. The mythical king of Phrygia, Midas, sent his throne to the sanctuary at the beginning of the 7th century BC, from far off Gordion in the heart of Asia Minor, to show his piety to Apollo. Another king, Gyges of Lydia, ancestor of Croesus, sent gold kraters, silver offerings and pure gold from Sardis about 675 BC. In Greece, the tyrant Kypselus of Corinth, who was renowned for his wealth, built the first treasury at Delphi and other leaders and cities followed his example. These small buildings, constructed on a temple plan, multiplied to decorate the sanctuary and cover the smaller precious offerings. In the mid-6th century BC a descendent of Gyges, Croesus, king of Lydia, consulted the Oracle because he had been assured of its supremacy before attacking the Persians (see above) and sent many rich gifts. Among other gold and silver offerings was a pure gold lion weighing 250 kilos set on a pyramid of 117 blocks of white gold (an amalgam of gold and silver). Two huge kraters, one gold and one silver were put each side of the temple entrance. Croesus, Amasis of Egypt and the Greeks themselves put large sums towards the construction of a new larger temple after the destruction of the earlier one by fire in 548 BC. It cost 300 talents (billions of drachmas today). The Alcmaeonids, exiled from Athens by the Peisistratids at this time, took over the work of reconstruction and paid out of their own pocket to put Parian marble in the façade instead of the cheaper poros which the contract specified.

The Classical Period (5th and 4th centuries BC)

During the Persian War in 480 BC Delphi was saved from attack by the miraculous intervention of Apollo. A huge rock tubled down from the Phaidriades and the Persians fled panic stricken. This famous victory by relatively few Greeks over thousands of Persians was attributed by the pious victors to the help of Apollo, and perhaps not unjustly, because training for the Games was a part of Greek religion, as is mentioned in the Homeric Hymn to Apollo Delios: "The Ionians with their long chitons assemble to honour you and... in each contest they entertain you, Apollo, with boxing and dancing and singing". The results of training body and soul appeared in the contest for freedom. E. N.Gardiner observes, "The victory of the Greeks over the Persians... was the victory of a handful of trained athletes against hordes of soft barbarians".

The Athenians, the greatest victors of the Persian War, dedicated the famous Treasury of the Athenians and the Stoa of the Athenians to Apollo after their victory of the Battle of Marathon. Other Greeks made equally brilliant gifts. A colossal statue of Apollo was set up after the sea-battle of Salamis and a wonderful golden tripod after the Battle of Plataea, inscribed with the names of the thirty-one Greek cities who defeated the army of the Great King. Delphi now began to mint silver coins.

In the mid-5th century BC the Phocians took over the sanctuary with Athenian help. This caused the S e c o n d S a c r e d W a r 448-446 BC ending in the

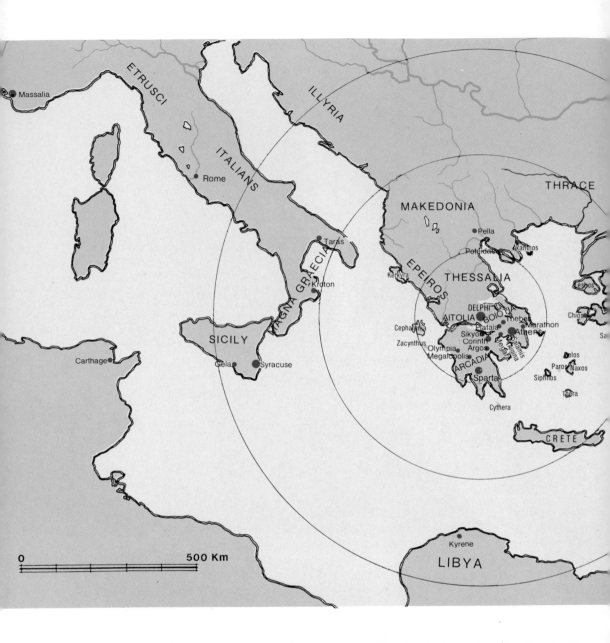

return of the sanctuary to the Delphians with Spartan help. In 373 BC the Apollo Temple was destroyed when huge rocks fell on it as the result of an earthquake. Its reconstruction began immediately under the supervision of naopes and the cost was met by the Delphians and the Amphictyonic League with a special tax per head (epikephalos obolos) and also by the rest of Greece. The calculations and costs are inscribed on a marble stele (Room 8 in the Museum). However, the reconstruction of the temple was interrupted by a new Sacred War.

The Third Sacred War 356-346 BC arose from the eternal strife between the Delphians and the other Phocians. The latter occupied the sanctuary

14

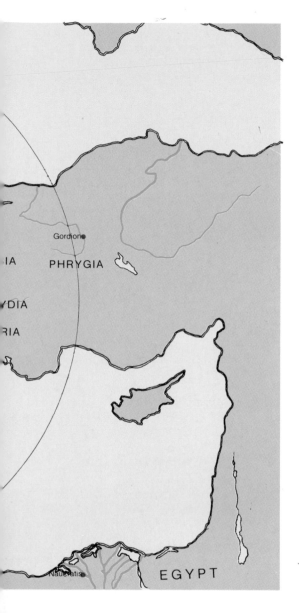

Gordion●

IA   PHRYGIA

DIA

RIA

Naucratis   EGYPT

Delphi, at the centre of the ancient world, and the most important cities that consulted the Oracle and either built or sent offerings.

again for about ten years, seized the revenues and melted down the precious offerings. The rest of Greece was horrified and Philip II of Macedon took the opportunity to intervene, with the result that the Phocians were defeated, ejected from the Amphictyonic League and compelled to pay a fine of 420 talents.

The Fourth Sacred War 340-338 BC was against the Locrians of Amphissa and ended in Philip of Macedon strengthening his hold on Greece after the Battle of Chaeronea 338 BC and taking over the two Phocian votes in the Amphictyonic League. At his instigation Delphi now minted silver staters which had Apollo on the omphalos on one side and Demeter on the other.

15

The prosperity of Delphi did not suffer much during the two 4th century Sacred Wars; on the contrary this century was still a golden age for the growth of the sanctuary. During this period the new temple of Athena Pronaia was built as well as the Tholos, the Gymnasium, the Treasuries of Thebes and Cyrene, the Stadium, etc.

The Hellenistic Period

The structure of the Greek world was radically altered under the Macedonian kings. Instead of city-states, the Amphictyonic League, colonies, allies, etc., the Hellenistic period is characterised by large kingdoms. The Greeks had widened man's horizons with poetry, philosophy, drama, etc., but Alexander the Great had widened the horizons of the world. Thus he created a unified cultural area, where the old beliefs warred with the new political conditions and fused into new religious and philosophical conceptions. The great sanctuaries of the Hellenistic world were now centres of dynastic propaganda. Outside the large kingdoms some traditional institutions continued their life.

One of these institutions, the Aetolian League, gained prestige by a victory over the Galatians who were attacking Delphi which, with the miraculous help of Apollo, was saved again, but now the Aetolians were the new masters of the sanctuary and inaugurated a yearly festival, the Salvation Festival, to preserve the memory of their great victory. They dedicated their Galatian plunder in their huge stoa outside and immediately west of the sanctuary. The kings of Pergamon showed their respect to Apollo.

After his victory over the Galatians in Asia Minor, Attalos I gave many gifts, including a stoa with paintings, scores of statues, an "oikos", a covered exedra, etc... Eumenes II and Attalos II gave large sums to learning and the arts, to the completion of the theatre and to the organisation of the festivals, the Eumeneia and the Attaleia.

The Attalids also took care to set up their statues in a prominent position in the sanctuary.

The most famous of the Macedonian gifts is the offering of Krateros. Perseus, the last king of Macedon, was preparing to set up his statue on a high column in front of the temple but, after his defeat by the Roman general, Aemilius Paulus, at Pydna in 168 BC, the victor set up his own equestrian statue on the same column. The Romans had become masters of the sanctuary in 191 BC and introduced the Roman pantheon and their own festival.

Delphi under the Romans

The nominal protection of Rome was not sufficient to protect Delphi from voracious plundering, even at the hands of the emperors themselves. It was plundered by the Maidoi of Thrace one winter and in 86 BC Sulla seized all the remaining precious offerings, which had survived so many centuries. The Maidoi burnt the temple and, for the first time in hundreds of years, the holy flame in the shrine went out.

Augustus took the sanctuary under his protection again, re-organised the Amphictyonic League and initiated the worship of the emperors in the Tholos in the Pronaia. Nevertheless, the city of Delphi was gradually deserted. Later Nero carried off five hundred statues but, on the other hand, Domitian repaired the temple. Plutarch spent more than twenty years at Delphi (105-126 AD) as a priest of Apollo and tried to resurrect the ancient cult. Hadrian and Antoninus later did the same. Herodes Atticus included Delphi in his generosity, setting up stone seats in the Stadium, not marble ones, as Pausanias noted on his visit to Delphi in 170 AD, when he found the sanctuary neglected, but still rich in treasures and works of art. Enough remained to be taken later to Constantinople by Constantine the Great and Theodosius. The Edict of Jan.10 381 AD struck the last blow at the worship of Apollo and the ancient religious tradition gave way to Christianity. Churches were built at Delphi, such as the Early Christian Basilica, whose mosaic floor can be seen in front of the Museum. According to legend, when Julian the Apostate sent Oreibasios to consult the Oracle, the Pythia gave her last melancholy utterance, a funeral epigram to the old religion:

> Tell the king, the fair-wrought hall has fallen to the ground.
> No longer has Phoebus a hut, nor a prophetic laurel.
> Nor a spring that speaks. The water of speech even is quenched.

(Translation by H.W.Parke, The Delphic Oracle).

THE MONUMENTS*

The Recent Archaeological History of the Site

Delphi did not cease to live in one sense or another in Byzantine and later times. The monastery of the Dormition of the Virgin, where the English traveller Edward Dodwell was offered hospitality, was on top of the ruined palaestra in the Gymnasium. It was removed by the French for their excavations, as were also the churches of St. John and St. George near the Apollo Temple. Most of the area of the sanctuary was taken up by the village of Kastri, which was also moved to its present position and renamed Delphi. From 150 AD onwards travellers called at Delphi, historians and archaeologists of every nationality, such as Cyriacus of Ancona (1436), Spon and Wheler (1676), Chandler (1766), Dodwell (1805), Holland (1812) and Gell (1819). Important information was noted by the Englishman W.M.Leake (1806) and the Germans, Thiersch (1840) and Ulrichs, who became a professor at Athens University.

One of the first to start excavating was the German K. Otfrid Müller with his student Ernst Curtius. In 1860 the Frenchmen, Wescher and Foucart, investigated the polygonal retaining wall and published inscriptions found in the basements and courtyards of the old village. Twenty years later the Frenchman Haussoulier uncovered part of the Stoa of the Athenians and, in 1887, the German Pomtow excavated the entrance to the sanctuary and carried out important topographical research. The interest of the Archaeological Service of the then newly constituted state of Greece was manifested from 1861, and in 1870, after an earthquake had destroyed the old village, efforts began to move it to a new site. Greek archaeologists (Dragoumis and Kastorchis) dug the site of Kastalia. The Americans and Germans sought permission to excavate the whole site but eventually it was granted to the French School of Archaeology in Athens in 1891 under the directorship of Théophile Homolle and systematic excavations began in 1892, together with the removal of the village. The results of the excavations are mostly published in the journal of the French School, the Bulletin de Correspondence Hellénique and in the volumes of the series Fouilles de Delphes, which is still being added to. Among the Greek archaeologists who have worked at Delphi the unforgettable Anthony Keramopoullos and Christos Karouzos (whose mother came from Delphi) rendered important services before the Second World War, when the archaeological office for the area was at Thebes. The author was the first Ephor of Antiquities to have his headquarters at Delphi in 1944. He concentrated on rescue work, as did Alexander Kondoleon, who died in April 1942, so that the antiquities and the Museum were spared the ravages of war and occupation. The large archaeological site of Delphi is divided in two by the Spring of Kastalia: to the east is the Sanctuary of Athena Pronaia, the Gymnasium, the east cemetery, etc.; to the west is the Sanctuary of Apollo, the Stadium, the ruins of the city, the west cemetery, etc.. The Sanctuary of Athena Pronaia, situated before the Apollo Temple, was the first sanctuary the ancient visitor came to and so received its name "Pronaia" (before the temple). Pausanias, the 2nd century AD traveller, begins his description of Delphi from the Pronaia Sanctuary (Pausanias, Guide to Greece X.8.6).

*The numbers in bold type in brackets refer to the corresponding plans of the Pronaia, the Gymnasium and the Sunctuary of Apollo.

The Sanctuary of Athena Pronaia

The usual name for the area is Marmaria (the Marbles) because of the ancient marble remains. It is a sloping area which was terraced in antiquity. The earliest remains are Mycenaean: clay female figurines (on show in the Museum) perhaps come from the shrine of a female deity, a predecessor of Athena.

The ancient east entrance is now closed and it is necessary to descend from the direction of Kastalia by a winding path, before reaching the east end of the sanctuary where the tour begins, as it did in antiquity.

Pausanias first noted the more important shrines in the sanctuary, which were still preserved in his time, and then recalls the shrine there of the hero Phylacos, who, according to legend, took part in the war against the Persians. He fought at the side of another hero, Autonoos, who had a shrine near Kastalia under Hyampeia, as Herodotus recounts. The two heroes amazed the Persians by their gigantic stature and thus put them to flight. Starting at the northwest entrance of the Pronaia Sanctuary there are two buildings (**1-2**) built on a temple plan, that is with a pronaos (vestibule) and a sekos (inner room). Only the polygonal stone foundations are preserved. The dimensions of the smaller are 4.85 by 3.95 m, the larger 6.10 by 8 m. They lie on a higher terrace between retaining walls and are entered from the south. It was thought that this was the shrine of Phylacos, but, because of their likeness to the Treasuries (**4-5**) (for example the similar layout, dimensions and positions, with the smaller behind the larger), it is now thought that they were probably treasuries, which were abandoned for some reason and replaced by the two more ornate ones (**4-5**).

The area between the two pairs of temples is, as is known today, the most ancient sacred place in Marmaria. Remains of Mycenaean worship were found here and it was here too that one of the oldest and most magnificent Greek temples was built for Athena about 650 BC. It was a poros peripteral in the Doric order. Twelve of its capitals, of the earliest known Doric architecture, and parts of

*Plan of the sanctuary of Athena Pronaia. **1-2.** Archaic treasuries. **3.** Archaic temple of Athena Pronaia. **4.** Doric treasury. **5.** Ionic treasury of the Massaliots. **6.** The Tholos. **7.** Later temple of Athena Pronaia. **8.** House of the Priests.*

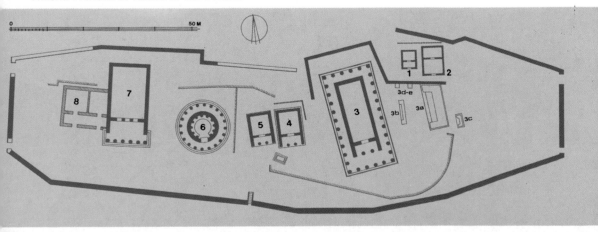

The Tholos in the Sanctuary of Pronaia.

its columns were found in the foundations of the second Archaic temple, which was built on top of it. They are now lined up on the west side.

The Second Archaic Temple (**3**) was built about 500 BC. It is a large peripteral temple also in the Doric order (27.45 by 13.25 m), whose plan was dictated by the narrowness of its site sq that the columns on the ends are only half the number of those on the long sides, ie. 6 by 12. The pronaos is composed of two columns *in antis* (between pilasters). There was no opisthodomos (back chamber) behind the sekos as there was no room. The temple was damaged in the Persian War and also in the earthquake in 373 BC. The three columns which are still preserved at the south-east corner have 4th century BC isodomic strengthening walls between

The restored part of the Tholos.

them, probably built after the earthquake. In March 1905 torrential rains caused a rockfall from Hyampeia which destroyed ten of the then remaining columns. In 1977 the Greek Archaeological Service used special technicians and broke and removed these rocks. The preserved pedimental and metope sculptures are kept in the Museum.

To the east of the Athena Temple are the remains of a large rectangular altar (**3a**) of the 6th century BC, which has a smaller altar on each of its long sides (**3b-c**). Between the altars **3a** and **3c** are three upright stelai, perhaps belonging to three offering tables, dedicated, according to the inscriptions, to *Zeus Polieus, Athena Ergane and Athena Zosteria.* The first inscription was found by A.Keramopoullos south of the temple in 1907. Two other built altars on the retaining wall belong to the goddesses *Hygeia* and *Eileithyia* (**3d-e**), according to the inscriptions on the wall.

After a glance at the well-built retaining walls the visitor should proceed to the treasuries (**4-5**) which are built of Parian marble. The larger, the Doric Treasury, (7.30 by 10.40 m) has two columns *in antis* and was built immediately after the Persian War. The smaller, the Massaliote Treasury, which is in the Ionic order (6.37 by 8.63 m) and considered slightly older, equalled the Siphnian Treasury in the Apollo Sanctuary in beauty. The two columns *in antis* have "aeolic" capitals decorated with palm leaves. Small parts of the outside frieze survive. This treasury was offered by the people of Marseille, who were Greek colonists from Phocaia, a city in Asia Minor. In the sekos a base for the statues of Roman emperors is still preserved.

Around the two treasuries are different bases with deep grooves in for setting up inscribed stelai. An inscribed base from a statue of the emperor Hadrian was found by A.Keramopoullos, built into the south side of the enclosure wall. The large rectangular base set obliquely to the two treasuries was perhaps for a trophy or other dedication from the Delphians, after the gods helped to drive back the Persians in 480 BC. C.Karouzos praises the arrangement of this monument: "The architectural picture of these monuments (as of others in the sanctuary) is not that of a lifeless row, but that of an animated group of statues, each with its own expression and movement". (C. Karouzos, *Delphi,* Athens 1974 p.65).

The circular Tholos (**6**) with its three restored columns dominates the ruins of Marmaria, as it must have in antiquity, because of its original circular appearance and the high standard of its decoration. It belongs to the decade 390-380 BC, a few years before the great earthquake, and its architect is thought to be Theodore from Phocaia in Asia Minor. He wrote a book on its excellence; he could be the same person as the architect Theodotos, who built the tholos at Epidauros a little later. The Tholos at Delphi has a diameter of 13.50 m and is built mostly of Parian

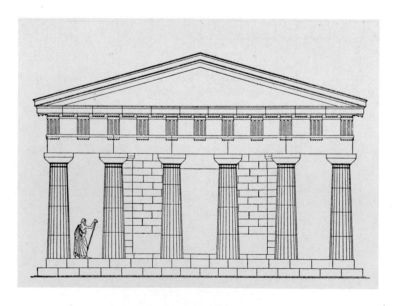

Reconstruction of the poros temple of Athena Pronaia (R. Demangel).

marble on a krepis of three steps; twenty Doric columns outside supported the entablature and the lower roof of the circular colonnade. The metopes were decorated with sculptured reliefs of the Battles of the Amazons and the Centaurs. Another row of smaller metopes high on the outer wall of the colonnade portrayed the exploits of Theseus and the Labours of Heracles. The threshold of the entrance on the south side of the circular sekos is preserved, while the floor, of stone from Eleusis, is partly restored. Round the wall of the sekos inside are ten Corinthian half columns. The conical roof had marble tiles and akroteria. Parts of the architectural and sculptured decoration of the Tholos are on show in the Museum, but details, such as the Lesbian moulding running round the bottom of the wall and other mouldings, are still *in situ.*

The purpose of the Tholos is unknown and Pausanias, unfortunately, does not mention the wonderful building. It has been suggested that it was for the worship of a chthonic goddess, as also the similar circular buildings at Epidauros, Olympia, the Athenian Agora, etc..

On the right of the Tholos is a later temple to Athena Pronaia (**7**) built to replace the archaic temple (3), which was destroyed in the earthquake in 373 BC. It is constructed of local limestone, from the quarries of Prophetes Elias, in the Doric order (22.60 by 11.55 m) with six Doric columns, on the façade only (a prostyle temple). It, too, has no opisthodomos, but it has a wider façade with two columns in the passage from the pronaos to the sekos; the metopes were undecorated. A base stood in the sekos in Roman times.

On the west side of the temple (**7**) lay an older building (**8**) 12.05 by 10.90 m. A prodomos running the width of the building gives entry to two rooms of about the same size, next to each other. Its polygonal walls date the building to the Archaic Period. Its purpose is uncertain but it is conventionally called the "House of the Priests". About 10m to the west is the narrow west end of the enclosure wall of the Pronaia Sanctuary with an exit in the southwest corner to the nearby Gymnasium.

Reconstruction of the Tholos in the sanctuary of Athena Pronaia (H. Pomtow).

The Gymnasium

As is usual in Greece there is a myth attached to the Gymnasium: Odysseus was gored in the leg by a boar, while hunting here with the sons of Autolykos, and this old wound enabled his maid, Eurykleia, to recognise him when he returned to Ithaca. So here at the foot of Hyampeia, not far from the sacred Kastalian spring, the young men of Delphi trained on a track renowned because of a Homeric hero, the wily Odysseus. In mythical times this steep hillside must have been covered with thick undergrowth.

In ancient Greece the Gymnasium was used for many facets of education which are taught nowadays in schools, colleges, by military training, etc.. The area had to be landscaped to accomodate its many installations, such as race-tracks, terraces, stairs, a drainage and sewage system. The Gymnasium at Delphi lies on two terraces with the palaestra on the lower level and the xystos on the upper.

The palaestra (**1**) is a building with a square peristyle inner court (the sides are 13.85 m long) with eight columns a side holding up the roof of stoa. On the south and west sides are rooms of different dimensions, lay-out and purpose. The large room on the west side was probably the dressing room; on the north side one room was the konima or konisterion. Fine sand was kept here, which was used by the athletes with oil to annoint their bodies. Another room was a sphairisterion, where the boxers and pankratiasts trained with sandbags. The room on the west side, built on a temple plan with two columns at the entrance, an ante-chamber and a main room, possibly contained a statue of one or more of the gods connected with the Gymnasium (Hermes, Heracles) against the wall. This was perhaps the Ephebion or Exedra. In good weather training took place in the open court, in bad weather in the stoa. In later times the church of the Panayia (**2**) was built here and on one of its columns - in fact a Gymnasium column re-used - Lord Byron and his friend Hobhouse carved their names in 1809.

Plan of the Gymnasium. **1.** *The Palaistra.* **2.** *The Katholikon of the Monastery of the Dormition.* **3.** *The reservoir.* **4.** *The baths.* **5.** *The Xystos (covered exercise area).* **6.** *The Paradromis.*

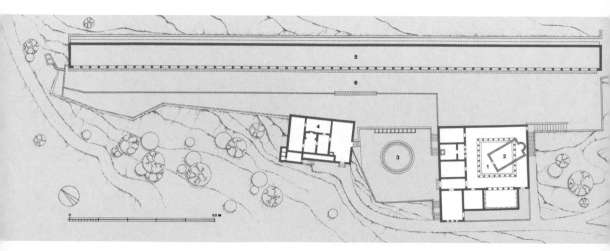

The Gymnasium.

On the west side of the palaestra a bath with three steps is relatively well preserved (**3**). On a retaining wall to the north are the remains, partly restored, of a marvellous fountain with eleven spouts and ten basins beneath them. The water came from Kastalia and drained into the circular bath. This was necessary in a Gymnasium so that the athletes could wash in cold water. A little further west there were warm baths provided with a hypocaust (**4**), which were constructed, along with two others in the Apollo Sanctuary, about 120 AD for the more demanding Romans.

On the upper terrace of the Gymnasium the *xystos* (**5**) can be seen, when the area is not overgrown. It is a huge colonnade running north-south and is longer than all the other palaestra buildings since it must have been about the length of a Delphic stade. The inner dimensions are 184.43 by 7.50 m. The colonnade was first constructed with poros columns in the Doric order but these were replaced in Roman times by marble Ionic ones on tall cubic bases. In order to be completely flat and solid the floor was scraped and thus the building was called a xystos (meaning scraped). The athletes trained here on the track on both wet and fine days. In good weather the *paradromis* was also used, a track outside and parallel to the stoa of the xystos (**6**). During Hellenistic times and later the area of the Gymnasium was frequented by every type of teacher, poet, philosopher, orator, musician, etc.. In the festival of the Eumenaia a torch race began from the Gymnasium and ended in front of the Apollo Temple.

In the neighbourhood of the Gymnasium was an important sanctuary to Demeter. Pausanias does not mention it, perhaps because it was only separated from the Gymnasium by a small wall (teichion, as the inscriptions call it). It was located at the southeast end of the xystos by J.Jannoray, but in 1980 G.Roux, using inscriptions and other excavated material, placed it at the northwest end where, during excavation, small finds and other remains of cult were found in the rocks. He supposes that an ancient shrine to Demeter may have extended as far as the other side of the Kastalian stream.

The Spring of Kastalia

Above the Gymnasium is the Spring of Kastalia, of great importance to the site: Pindar rightly said that water was one of nature's best gifts. In antiquity the natural spring sufficed for a local cult, before man interfered; but the Greeks embellished even nature. There are two fountains. The archaic fountain was found by chance in 1959 when the road was broadened. It was partly restored in 1969 and 1977 and finally published by the Director of the French School of Archaeology, Pierre Amandry (1977). It is a poros construction dating to the first Sacred War (600-590 BC). The water, rising at the base of Hyampeia, ran without pipes down to the fountain 50 m lower. About 460 BC a channel was constructed, partly cut in the rock, and covered with thick tiles. This channel was finally uncovered in 1977. The water collected in a built cistern with dimensions of about 6.5 by 1.5 m and fell from there through four lionshead spouts. The façade of the fountain was stuccoed and painted; traces of blue paint survive. The paved court in front (now partly restored) had benches around and a wall with high orthostates. Proceeding fifty metres towards the Cliff of Hyampeia cuttings can be seen in the rock, from which the water emerges, and, on the left, the narrow cleft between the Phaidriades. The water is always cold and good to taste, if drunk immediately from the spring. The second fountain was made in Hellenistic or Roman times, when the rock was cut and a small square levelled, in front of which were eight rock-cut steps. Beyond is the narrow rock-cut water cistern roughly one metre by half a metre. The water falls from the right and meets a sluice on the left which controls its level so that it flows through the seven spouts or so that the cistern can be emptied for cleaning. The spouts were probably decorated with lion or gorgon heads. The surrounding rock was covered with upright marble slabs to a height of 2.50 m. while higher up niches were cut in the cliff to receive offerings varying from figurines to biscuits. The small column drum in the large niche was used as an altar support in the later Christian shrine, where the worshippers lit their candles until recently.

Although the architectural details of the fountains are mentioned here for today's archaeological visitors, they certainly did not interest the ancient worshippers who came to the sacred place with a religious awe, for not only the Pythia, but everyone else, including the priests, had to purify themselves here before entering the sanctuary or Apollo Temple to sacrifice, consult the oracle, or carry out any other religious ceremony. Near the archaic fountain to the east are the possible remains of the shrine to the hero Autonoos, mentioned with Phylacos above. He

The modern spring of Kastalia.

helped twice to save the sanctuary from foreign invasion, once from the Persians and once from the Galatians.

The Apollo Sanctuary

In antiquity the town of Delphi and the higher Apollo Sanctuary covered almost the whole area visible from the Pronaia under the cliff of Rodini, ancient Nauplia. The appearance of this semi-circular place must have been fabulous when all the buildings were still standing surrounded by the "sacred wall of Apollo" as Pausanias called the sanctuary wall, which he describes after the Pronaia Temple and the Kastalian Spring.

This enclosure wall would be outstanding on its own for its craftsmanship, if it did not happen to contain so many other wonderful antiquities. It encompasses a steeply descending trapezoidal stretch (greatest dimensions 195 by 135 m) and was landscaped as early as the Archaic Period. It was repaired in the 5th and 4th centuries BC but its dimensions remained almost unchanged throughout its history, except for the 3rd century BC additions of the Stoa of the Aetolians to the west and the offerings of Attalos I in the east. The sanctuary was entered from the east (A,B,C,D,E) and west (A´,B´,C´,D´,E´) but the main entrance, which is used today, was in the southeast corner, where the Sacred Way begins.

The tiled square outside the main entrance is the **Roman Agora** and betrays its Roman construction, especially on the north side where there were shops at the back of the Ionic stoa, in which suppliants and visitors could buy small offerings to Apollo, such as figurines, small vases and tripods, etc.. Later on splendid processions were held here during the Pythian Games. Plinths and bases, some of which are preserved, supported statues of Roman emperors and other important people. The columns of the stoa have been recently restored (1977) and marble architectural fragments have been assembled in the stoa and shops together with Early Christian.

The level of the present day entrance to the sanctuary is a little higher than the ancient one and the first part of the paving of the Sacred Way belongs to the years of decline.

On entering the sanctuary the visitor should remember its sanctity while enjoying its view. Moreover, he will find that at each change of position he will get a different picture of the monuments, whether he is looking at them as a group or at each one separately. Nowhere else have so many original works of art been

The roman agora.

assembled in their true surroundings and in such a small area. The whole sanctuary was full of votive offerings to delight the god (the ancient Greek word for statue
was agalma, which literally meant an object of delight). Immediately past the
entrance is the first stone base which belongs to the Cercyraion Bull (**1**). Every
offering has a myth or historical fact attached to it and that of the Cercyraion Bull
will be told as an example. According to Pausanias (X.9.3) a bull in Cercyra
(Corfu) left his field, went down to the sea and bleated on the shore. This occurred
every day so finally the herdsman went to see what was wrong and saw a huge
number of tunny fisch in the sea. He went and told the inhabitants of Cercyra in the
town and they tried in vain to catch the fish. Finally they sent to Delphi to ask what
they should do and the Pythia told them to sacrifice the bull to the god of the sea.
As soon as they had carried out this sacrifice to Poseidon they were able to catch
the fish, which they sold at a vast profit as there were so many, and, with a tenth of
this, they offered a bronze bull at Olympia and another at Delphi. Pausanias
probably heard this story from a contemporary guide. The base for the bull's statue
is 4 by 5.20 m but it was originally taller than it is today and, together with the
statue, it must have been very imposing. The bull was made in the decade 490-
480 BC by the Aeginetan sculptor, Theopropos, but, according to the inscription

General view of the Apollon Sanctuary.

THE SANCTUARY OF APOLLO

1. Cercyraian Bull
2. Offering of the Arcadians
3. Spartan Monument
4. Trojan Horse
5. Athenian Offering
6. The Seven against Thebes
7. The Epigonoi
8. The Kings of Argos
9. Hellenistic Monument
10. Bronze Statue of Philopoemen
11-12. Two bases
13-14. Two niches
15. Tarentine Monument
16. Sicyonian Treasury
17. Statues from Cnidos
18. Aetolian Offering
19. Siphnian Treasury
20. Liparian Offering
21. Theban Treasury
22. Niche
23. Boeotian Treasury
24. Megarian Treasury
25. Syracusan Treasury
26. Treasury of Klazomenae
27. Treasury of Cnidos
28α. The stone Omphalos
28. Potidaean Treasury
29. Unidentified archaic Treasury
30. The Treasury of the Athenians
31. The Asclepieion
32. Archaic fountain
33. The Bouleuterion
34. Exedra of Herodes Atticus
35. The Spring of Ge
36. The Rock of Sibylle
37. Boeotian Offerings
38. Exedrae
39. Monument with three columns
40. Unidentified archaic Treasury
41. The Naxian Sphinx
42. The Stoa of the Athenians
43. Corinthian Treasury
44. Treasury of Cyrene
45. The Prytaneion
46. Unidentified archaic Treasury
47. Treasury of Brasidas and the Acanthians
48. Tarantine Monument (second).

49. The Tripod of Plataea
50. The Chariot of Rhodes
51. Unidentified archaic Treasury
52. Offering of the Messenians
53. The Aemilius Paulus Monument
54. Stoa of Attalos I
55. The «oikos» of Attalos («Dionysion»)
56. Offerings of Attalos I
57. Statue of Attalos I
58. Statue of Eumenes II
59. Unidentified Treasury
60. The Altar of Chios
61. Bronze palm tree
62. The monument of Aristaineta
63. The pedestal of the statue of Prusias
64. Apollo Sitalcas
65. The Tripods of the Deinomenids
66. Kassotis Spring
67. Statues of the Aitolian Generals
68. Cercyraian base
69. Horse-shoe shaped base
70. The Offering of Daochos II
71. Archaic polygonal wall
72. The Acanthus Column with dancing caryatids
73. Base of unidentified offering
74. «Temenos of Neoptolemos»
75. The Stone of Kronos
76. 4th century B.C. monument
77. The Cnidian Clubhouse
78. Supposed Messenian Offering
79. Temple of Apollo
80. Shrine of the Muses
81-85. Unidentified archaic Treasuries
86-87. Statue bases
88. The Offering of Krateros
89-90. The great Stoa of the Aitolians
91. Unidentified Treasury
92. The Theatre
93-94. Unidentified Treasuries
95. The Poteidanion

89

90

N

0   10

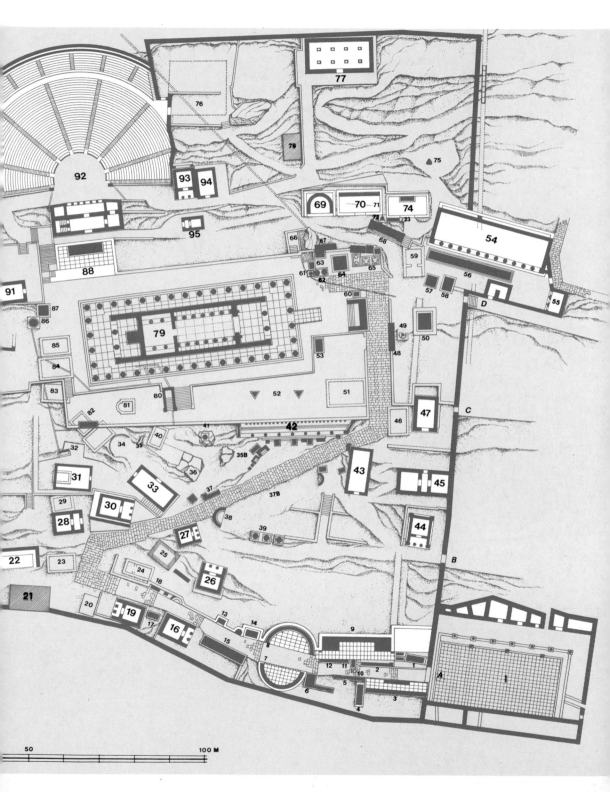

50   100 M

31

on its north side (above left), the base was made in the 4th century BC.

Further on an oblong base 9.40 m long supported the Offering of the Arcadians (**2**). Its inscription corrects Pausanias, who notes that it was an offering from the Arcadian city of Tegea only. Above this base stood a line of nine bronze statues: Apollo, Nike (Victory), Callisto (mythical mother of the eponymous hero, Arcas), Arcas (founder of the Arcadians) and his children, Elatos, Areidas, Azan, Triphylos and Erasos. The offering was made after the Arcadians attacked Laconia with their ally the Theban general, Epaminondas in 369 BC.

On the left opposite the Arcadian offering was the Spartan Monument (**3**) consisting, according to Pausanias, of 38 bronze statues by different craftsmen. Among others Lysander was depicted being crowned by Poseidon, the Dioscuri, Zeus, Apollo, Artemis and the Spartan generals and admirals who, under Lysander, defeated the Athenians at the great naval battle of Aegospotami in 404 BC, the final year of the Peloponnesian War. Pausanias gives their names. This monument of "the admirals" was set up after the defeat of the Athenians next to their already existing monument (below no. 5).

The Argives offered the Trojan Horse (**4**) made of bronze, whose base is next to that of the Spartan admirals. It was made by the Argive sculptor, Antiphanes, as an offering to Apollo from the spoils of their victory over the Spartans at the Battle of Thyreatis 414 BC.

The Athenian Offering (**5**) already mentioned, which is earlier than that of the Peloponnesians and later only than the Cercyraion Bull, is the first of a series of Athenian offerings which line the Sacred Way. It depicts Miltiades, the victor of the Battle of Marathon, with the deities of Delphi and Athens, ie. Apollo and Athena, and the seven eponymous heroes of the Attic tribes. The offering was not made immediately after Marathon, but after his honours had been restored to Miltiades, perhaps by his son Cimon, about 460 BC. Much later the three eponymous kings of the new tribs, Antigonos of Macedon, his son, Demetrius Polyorketes and another Macedonian king, Ptolemy of Egypt, were added to the seven eponymous heroes of the Attic tribes. West of the Athenian offering and that of the Trojan

Reconstruction of the Bull of the Corcyraeans (H. Pomtow).

Horse was another Argive offering: the Seven against Thebes (**6**). The seven mythical Argive leaders are depicted making war on Eteocles of Thebes, who had Amphiaraos in his chariot, which was driven by Baton. The offering was set up after the Athenian and Argive victory against the Spartans at Oinoe (west of Argos) in 456 BC. The statues were made by Hypatodoros and Aristogeiton.

On the same side there follows a further Argive offering set in a semi-circular space with a diameter of 12m, the Epigoni (**7**). They were the sons of the Seven against Thebes who, in contrast to their unlucky parents, captured and destroyed Thebes. The inscription, cut in large letters, briefly says: "The Argives offered to Apollo", but Pausanias notes that this offering was also set up after the victory at Oinoe in 456 BC.

Opposite the semi-circle of the Epigoni was another semi-circular Argive offering, the kings of Argos (**8**), consisting of ten bronze statues of heroes and mythical kings of Argos. First came Danaos with his daughter Hypermnestra, and other members of the family, ending with Alcmene and Heracles. The myth in which Alcmene gave birth to Heracles in Thebes united Argos and Thebes. This offering was meant to commemorate the link, but was made when the Argives needed Theban friendship after 370 BC. The monument, made by the Argive sculptor, Antiphanes, was set up after the foundation of the city of Messene in 369 BC, by the Argives and the Theban general, Epaminondas. Behind the monuments on the right side of the Sacred Way already described are the ruins of a Hellenistic Monument (**9**) with a rectangular niche. Nothing is known about this monument and, as it is almost invisible, it need not detain the visitor.

In front of this anonymous monument is the rectangular base of the bronze Statue of Philopoemen (**10**), a general of the Achaian League. The inscription reads that the Achaians set up the monument because Philopoemen was valiant and considerate. On the other hand, Plutarch writes that Philopoemen was depicted killing Machanidas, the Spartan tyrant, after the Battle of Mantineia 207 BC.

The following two bases (**11-12**) and the two niches (**13-14**) beyond the Argive offering (8) have not been identified and make a good point for the visitor to look

Reconstruction of the Tholos of the Sikyonians (H. Pomtow).

back on the first ten offerings on the Sacred Way, which must have contained over a hundred bronze statues of gods, demi-gods, mythical representations and historical personalities, generals, admirals, a bull, the Trojan Horse, groups of equestrian fighters and, probably, many other small offerings which have disappeared. They must have presented a wonderful picture of Greek mythology, religion, history and art.

Continuing up the Sacred Way part of the base of the Tarentine Monument (15) is preserved on the left together with part of the offering inscription. Taras was a Spartan colony in south Italy (Magna Graecia). After their victory against the Messapi at the beginning of the 5th century BC the Tarentines set up this monument from a tenth of the spoil. It depicted female prisoners and horses and was made by the famous Argive bronze sculptor, Ageladas.

The scenery changes with the ruins of the first Treasury, the Sicyonian Treasury (16). In antiquity the east side of this treasury, which is built on a temple plan with two columns *in antis,* would have been seen from the Sacred Way. Today only the ruins of its poros foundations remain, which re-use the poros circular and rectangular blocks from two earliet treasuries. The two older treasuries on the same site consisted of a tholos, with a diameter of 6.32 m and thirteen Doric columns round it, and a monopteros - a building with a roof supported by columns, but no sekos. It was about 4.20 by 5.50 m and had 4 by 5 Doric columns. The metopes on show in the Museum (Room 4) belong to this building. According to one version, the chariot, in which Cleisthenes, Tyrant of Sicyon, won the Pythian Games in 582 BC, was displayed in the monopteros. At about this time the circular treasury (the tholos) was set up. The later Sicyonian Treasury was built in 500 BC by the oligarchs who had pushed the Orthagorid tyrants out of Sicyon.

It is thought that statues from Cnidos (17) in Asia Minor stood between the Sicyonian and the following Siphnian Treasury (19), while opposite them, on the other side of the Sacred Way, was an Aetolian Offering (18).

The Siphnian Treasury (19) was one of the most beatiful buildings at Delphi. This small Aegean island reached its acme in the mid-6th century BC gathering wealth from its gold and silver mines. About 525 BC refugees from Samos, who had revolted against the tyranny of Polykrates, plundered the island, so it is thought that the treasury must have been constructed before this time. A part from the foundations, it is built, side by side with the Sicyonian Treasury, of beautiful Parian marble on the usual treasury plan of a megaron, facing west. At this point a small square, like a stair landing, is made by the Sacred Way turning a corner, while another flatter road comes from the south gate of the temple (A´). In antiquity the visitor to this Ionic treasury would first have admired the two female statues (caryatids), who supported the entablature and the pediment, and the carved frieze round the four sides of the building whose total length was 29.63 m. The preserved parts of the caryatid, frieze sculpture and pediment are in a special Museum show room (3).

Following the road towards the exit (A´), on the left is the Liparian Offering base (20). They inhabited the largest of the Aeolian Islands, north of Sicily. Further on are the ruins of the beautiful Theban Treasury (21), built after the Battle of Leuctra 371 BC with inscriptions of honour cut in its walls. Opposite is a worn base (22) in a rectangular niche and the remains of another older Boeotian Treasury (23) with names carved on the foundation stones.

Returning to the "stair landing" the Megarian Treasury (24) can be identified from the decrees of the city of Megara, which are carved on the restored wall in front of the treasury. It used to be thought that this treasury belonged to the

Reconstruction of the treasury of the Siphnians.

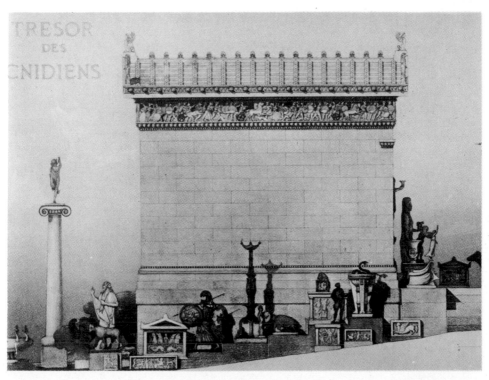

Syracusans but now a nearby one (25) is attributed to them. It was built after their victory over the Athenians in 413 BC opposite that of the Athenians. Few traces of the Megarian Treasury are preserved but a corner triglyph of black stone and a white marble geison belonging to the Doric Syracusan Treasury can be seen in the covered area in front of the Museum.

Near the Syracusan Treasury (**25**) were two treasuries belonging to cities in Asia Minor. That in the Aeolic order was perhaps the Treasury of Klazomenae (**26**) while near it is the Treasury of Cnidos (**27**) built in the Ionic order with fine architectural decoration in 550-545 BC with a tenth of the booty from some victory. This could have been the prototype of the Siphnian Treasury, as it also had caryatids.

Near the place where a stone omphalos (**28a**) has been set up from elsewhere is the supposed Potidaean Treasury (**28**) belonging to a town in the Chalcidic Peninsular; it was built of Poros about 500 BC. There are the few remains of another unidentified archaic treasury (**29**) close by. The Treasury of the Athenians (**30**) is one of the most famous offerings and, since its restoration, is perhaps the hallmark of the sanctuary at Delphi. It was worked on and restored (1903-06) by the French architect, Replat, at a cost of 35,000 gold drachmae, payed for by the city of Athens. It is built of Parian marble in the Doric order on the usual temple plan with columns *in antis*. It is 9.687 m long and 6.621 m wide. It had 30 sculptured metopes: the six on the façade show the Amazonomachy, the nine on the south side show the Labours of the Athenian hero, Theseus, the nine on the north side the Labours of Heracles, as also the six on the west side, where the theft of the cattle of Geryon is depicted. The 24 best preserved metopes are on show in the Museum (Room of the Athenian Treasury) and their gypsum replicas are in the restored building. The pediments above were also decorated with sculptured reliefs (Theseus and Perithous on the east and a battle scene on the west). There is some doubt whether the treasury was built before or (according to Pausanias) after the Battle of Marathon, but it is certain that Persian arms from this Athenian victory were displayed on a triangular base running along the south side on the outside, as a large inscription on the base relates. On the other hand, from the third century BC and onwards, inscriptions began to be cut on the walls, especially decrees honouring Athenian citizens. The inscriptions on the south wall are particularly interesting; carved between 138 and 128 BC, they consist of two hymns to Apollo with the ancient notes for voices and musical instruments. They are now in the Museum (Room 6).

Behind the Athenian Treasury at a lower level the ruins of a small unidentified archaic temple can be distinguished between the better preserved and partly restored ruins of the Asclepieion (**31**). A little to the north an archaic fountain (**32**) is fairly well preserved (somewhat restored in 1977). Next to the Athenian Treasury are the ruins of a relatively long, oblong, poros building, the Bouleuterion (**33**), recently partly restored. The fifteen councillors of the city of Delphi met here and made decisions.

Above the Bouleuterion, a little to the west, are the scarcely visible ruins of an unidentified archaic treasury, but the exedra can be seen which is assumed to be the offering of Herodes Atticus (**34**).

Nearby are some of the oldest and most holy ruins at Delphi. The Spring of Ge (**35**), owner of the sanctuary before Apollo, was guarded by the Pytho, whom Apollo killed. Themis, goddess of justice, and Poseidon, initially god of the freshwater underground streams, were also worshipped here. Nearby is the Rock of the Sibyl (**36**), known from Plutarch and Pausanias, which must have fallen from the Phaidriades thousands of years ago. In antiquity it was beleived the first Sibyl

The treasury of the Athenians.

The Sacred Way, the treasury of the Athenians, and the rock of the Sibyl.

TRESOR
DES ATHENIENS

FACADE PRINCIPALE

TRESOR
DES ATHENIENS

A. Tournaire

began to give oracles from here, when she came from Troy. Above the Sybilline Rock, to the north, a smaller rock is the so-called rock of Leto, as, according to the myth, Leto stood here holding the infant Apollo while he shot the Pytho. This is depicted on the clay akroteria of the temple of the Etruscan city of Veii in modern Lazio. The area surrounding these antiquities was destroyed when the Apollo Temple and its retaining wall were constructed after 548 BC.

In front of the Rocks of Sibyl and Leto is a line of different bases from Boeotian offerings (**37**). Opposite them on the other side of the Sacred Way, at an equal distance from the Bouleuterion (33) and the Prytaneion (45), lies the *Halos,* a place kept free of buildings for the Stepteria, a religious drama which was held every eight years. A portrayal of Apollo's killing of the Pytho took place: a child with both parents living, played the role of Apollo and members of the family of the Labyades took him up the Dolonia Stair with lighted torches; the child pointed to the serpent's nest and the torchbearers set it on fire. Then everyone left without looking back, as Apollo did when he fled to Tempe to be purified.

By this part of the Halos the chryselephantine objects, the silver bull and other finds were found under the paving of the Sacred Way in two pits in 1939. They are on show in a special room in the Museum (Room 5). Different monuments surround the area of the Halos, such as exedrae (**38**) and a monument with three columns (**39**), etc..

On the left of the Sacred Way are the ruins of an unidentified archaic treasury (**40**) and the base of the famous Naxian Sphinx (**41**) on show in the Museum (Room 3). Only many scattered pieces from the drums, with characteristic shallow grooves, of the column, on which the Sphinx stood, remain on the spot. It was more than 12m high.

On the same level looking towards the ascending Sacred Way is the long Stoa of the Athenians (**42**) with many bases down the length of the façade for the

Reconstruction of the stoa of the Athenians and the temple of the Alkmeonidai (P. Amandry).
◄*Reconstruction of the facade and the south side of the treasury of the Athenians (A. Tournaire).*

The Stoa of the Athenians.

The Sacred Way, with the Altar of the Chians on the right and the circular base for the tripod of the Plataeans on the left.

different offerings, including one Boeotian offering. The Stoa was constructed after 478 BC to house the spoils from the naval victories of the Athenians over the Persians. It was built in the Ionic order against the polygonal retaining wall for the embankment of the Apollo temple and was 30 m long, but only 4 m deep. On the façade between the pilasters stood eight thin fluted marble columns, each made from a single stone, which supported the wooden roof. On the stylobate the large lettered inscription, which is still legible, relates that the Athenians offered: a) the Stoa, b) the flax cables which held together the bridge of boats by which Xerxes' army crossed the Hellespont and c) the prows with bronze figureheads from the Persian ships. The polygonal retaining wall with its curving joints mentioned above is in itself a work of art and a monument to the knowledge of the ancient world. About eight hundred inscriptions are carved on it, most of them acts of manumission.

Opposite the east end of the Stoa of the Athenians on the right side of the

Sacred Way are the few remains of the oblong Corinthian Treasury (**43**) built near the Doloneian Stair. They are important as this treasury, which was perhaps built in the 7th century BC, is the oldest of the Delphic treasuries. Further east, at a lower level, near Gate B, is the possible Treasury of Cyrene (**44**) built in the Doric order on the usual plan with two columns *in antis*. To the north of this and on a higher terrace held by a retaining wall is the Prytaneion (Magistrates Hall) (**45**) built against the enclosure wall. It has an odd plan with two symmetrical rooms right and left of a corridor with an entrance to the north. Higher up the hill supported by another retaining wall are the ruins of an unidentified archaic treasury (**46**) and, next to it, the Treasury of Brasidas and the Acanthians (**47**) built after their victory against the Athenians at Amphipolis. Ascending the Sacred Way on the left is the short side of the polygonal retaining wall with its clear inscriptions and on the right, one behind the other, are the ruins of at least three important monuments. First is a second Tarrantine Monument (**48**) (see above (15) for the first) and behind it was the famous gold Tripod of Plataia (**49**) and the gold-plated Chariot of Rhodes (**50**). Only the circular base remains from the Tripod, which commemorated the victory of Plataia 479 BC, as the Phocians stole the Tripod during the Third Sacred War (357-346 BC). The column for the gold tripod bowl, made of three entwined bronze snakes, was taken to Constatinople by Constatine the Great and is still preserved there in the Hippodrome, with the names of the cities who took part in this victorious battle against the Persians. On the other hand, the large base belonging to the gilded Chariot of Rhodes dedicated in 304 BC can easily be seen.

Opposite the Monument of the Tarrantines (48) an opening in the polygonal wall leads to the embankment south of the Apollo Temple. There, lower down, are the ruins of another unidentified archaic treasury (**51**) and the supposed position of the double offering of the Messenians in Naupactos (**52**), two statues on triangular bases of Nike, like the Nike of Paionios at Olympia. Leaving the west part of the embankment for later, the Aemilius Paulus Monument (**53**) can be seen. It was being prepared as an offering by Perseus, the last king of Macedon, when this Roman general conquered him at the Battle of Pydna 168 BC. This battle not only brought about the end of Macedonian rule, but also involved the yielding of all Greece to the Romans. Thus, the victorious Aemilius Paulus set up his 12 m high equestrian statue on the base of his defeated opponent. This base with its sculptures of the Battle of Pydna is preserved and on show outside the Museum in front of the Offices. Returning to the Sacred Way, and ommitting for the moment the Altar of Chios (60) on the left, on the right were a number of monuments dedicated by the Attalids of Pergamon, accessible in antiquity also from the north Gates (D´,E´) in the enclosure wall. The large twostoried Stoa of Attalos (**54**), who died in 197 BC, was changed into a reservoir in the 4th century AD for the baths outside the sanctuary. The "House of Attalos" (**55**) is supposed to be the "Dionysion". A magnificent base for the Offerings of Attalos I (**56**) and two statue bases of Attalos I (**57**) and Eumenes II (**58**), who died in 159 BC, put up by the Amphictyonic League, complete the Attalid monuments. A few ruins from one more unidentified treasury (**59**) are preserved west of the Attalid offerings. Returning to the square in front of the Apollo Temple the Altar of Chios (**60**) lies on the left. This large altar, 8.60 by 5.10 m, was dedicated to Apollo in the 5th century BC, according to Herodotus and the inscription on it. For this the right of promanteia was given to the Chians (inscribed in the southeast corner). It was made from black marble, apart from the base and epistepsis, which were of white marble. Steps from the side of the temple lead up to it. It was repaired in the 3rd and 1st centuries BC and is now partly restored.

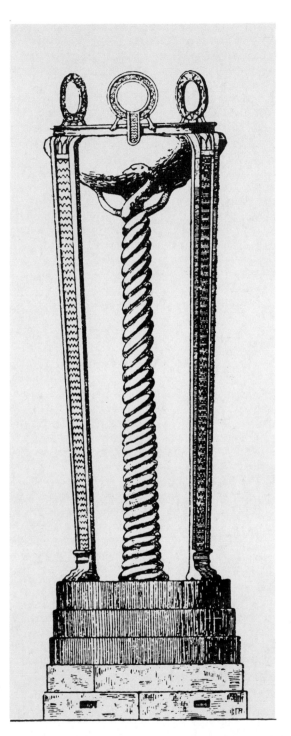

Reconstruction of the tripod of the Plataeans (Furtwaegler-Bulle).
Reconstruction of the base of the statue of Aemilius Paulus.

The north side of the square in front of the temple is crowded with monuments of different dates because of its important situation. From west to east are: the base for a bronze palm tree (**61**), which supported a gold-plated statue of Athena, an Athenian offering made after their victory over the Persians on the River Eurymedon; the bicolumnar monument of the lady Aristaineta (**62**); the high base for the statue of Prousias of Bithynia (**63**) dedicated, according to its inscription, by the Aetolian Confederacy; the very large base of the statue of Apollo Sitalkas (**64**) which was 16 m high, dedicated by the Amphictyonic League from the fine the Phocians paid. The epithet Sitalkas signifies Apollo's role as protector of grain so that the harvests should be good.

Three bases further east were for the gold Tripods of the Deinomenids (**65**), Hiero, Polyzalos and Trasyboulos, tyrants of Gela and Syracuse in Sicily. They were the sons of Deinomenes, Tyrant of Syracuse. The tripods were dedicated after the victory over the Carthaginians at Himera in 480 BC. The Phocians carried them off during the Third Sacred War. In the Museum is part of another offering made by Polyzalos, the famous bronze charioteer.

The Spring Kassotis, like the Kastalian Spring, played an important role in the ceremonial side of the cult, especially that of the oracle. In contrast to Kastalia, Kassotis (**66**) was only recently located behind the base of Prousias. It was believed that the waters plunged into the earth and flowed up again in the temple. The spring took its name from a nymph of Parnassos. Higher up behind the Deinomenid offerings are the statue bases of the Aetolian Generals (**67**) and another so-called Cercyraion base (**68**).

Further uphill is a row of important dedications which are now easily accessible as the area has been recently cleared. First is a horse-shoe shaped base (**69**), which supported at least seventeen Hellenistic marble statues. To the east is an oblong base belonging to the Offering of Daochos II (**70**), the Thessalian tetrarch, who was a hieromnemon of the Delphian Amphictyonic League (336-332 BC) and a friend of Philip II of Macedon. The inscribed bases of nine statues are preserved, belonging to Apollo, the donor, his ancestors and his son. The offering has recently been put together in the Museum by P.Themelis (Room 11). There are traces of an archaic polygonal wall (**71**) by the Daochos offering.

The Acanthus Column (**72**), an offering on a poros base with the letters PAN (krates), a well-known contractor from Delphi, is peculiar. It was 10.90 m high and supported a tripod with a bronze bowl, which was also supported on the heads of three caryatids dancing between the tripod feet. It was constructed about 350-320 BC and was probably an Athenian dedication. The dancers and column drums are on show in the Museum (Room 11). The rectangular base of another unidentified offering (**73**) is attached to the above.

Behind these bases is a spacious building known as the "Temenos of Neoptolemos" (**74**). Neoptolemos was the son of the Homeric hero Achilles who, according to legend, was killed by a priest of Apollo at Delphi and buried here. Higher up is roughly the place where the Stone of Kronos (**75**) was thought to have lain. This stone, which was not very big, according to Pausanias, received a daily libation of oil and other things, as it was believed to have been coughed up by Kronos, who had swallowed it instead of his son Zeus.

High up east of the Theatre are a few more noteworthy monuments, but they are often inaccessible because of the undergrowth. Near the upper row of the Theatre (**76**) are the ruins of a 4th century BC monument which was not finished. Higher still, attached to the north wall of the enclosure, are the remains of the famous Cnidian Clubhouse (**77**). A terrace was made to receive the rectangular hall 18.70 by 9.53 m, whose roof was supported by two rows of four wooden posts. It was entered from the south side and had a bench all round the walls. It owed its fame to the paintings by the famous Thasian artist, Polygnotos, which covered the walls. They were painted in the mid-5th century when the club was built. On the right of the entrance the Fall of Troy was depicted and on the left the Descent of Odysseus to Hades. These paintings were copied in vase painting and other art, and extant vases are examined to see if they bear a likeness to the work of Polygnotos, which is extensively described by Pausanias (X. 25.31). An inscription relates, however, that the paintings were touched up by three painters sent by Attalos I.

The east side of the temple of Apollo, with the ramp. The base of Prousias on the right.

Descending from the Cnidian Clubhouse to the Apollo Temple, among fallen rocks and retaining walls, are the remains of a base of a supposed Messenian Offering **(78)**.

This description of the monuments of the northeast corner digresses from the usual visitor's route but is necessary for a complete tour of the sanctuary. Returning now to the square in front of the Apollo Temple **(79)**, the visitor can see the remains of the building which must once have dominated the sanctuary. It has undergone centuries of successive catastrophes and rebuilding, but ancient authors and archaeological finds allow a fairly good reconstruction of its different appearances and the phases of its cult.

The last rebuilding occurred in the 4th century BC, but legend recounts that the first temple was a simple hut of laurel leaves from the Vale of Tempe. The second mythical temple was also made from material which came from the north: wax and

Restored columns of the temple of Apollo.

The temple of Apollo from the N.W.▶

Reconstruction of the 4th century B.C. temple (H. Schleif).

feathers (ptera giving the name of pterinos temple) sent by Apollo from the Hyper-boreans. The third temple was of bronze. The fourth and first historical temple was of poros and was built, with Apollo's help, by the mythical architects, Trophonios and Agamedes, according to a Homeric Hymn to Pythian Apollo. Excavated traces of it belong to the 7th century BC. Its architectural fragments have been found built into the back part of the polygonal retaining wall, at the spring (80), between this wall and the temple, and elsewhere. This temple was burnt in 548 BC and was shortly rebuilt. The new building was the so-called archaic temple or Alcmaeonid Temple, named after the noble Athenian family. The cost was met by gifts from the whole Greek world (and Amasis of Egypt) and from the contributions of the Amphictyonic League. The Alcmaeonids, who had been exiled by Peisistratos, were the contractors for the construction and paid more than their allotted share to construct the façade and the reliefs of the east pediment from Parian marble instead of poros (see below Museum Room 8). This temple was destroyed by an earthquake in 373 BC. Its reconstruction was delayed by the Third Sacred War (356-346 BC), but with the help of all Greece it was again rebuilt on the plan, and with almost the same dimensions, as the Alcmaeonid Temple, with six columns at the ends and fifteen down each side, that is with archaic proportions. It was finished about 330BC. Poros was used for the columns and entablature, while the rest was of black marble from Parnassos. The first architect was Spintharos of

Reconstruction of the façade of the temple of the Alkmeonidai (F. Courby).

Corinth, then, after his death, his co-citizens, Xenodoros and Agathon. The reliefs were made by the Athenian artists, Praxias and Androsthenes (see below Museum Room 7-8).

The present ruins belong to the 4th century BC temple. The foundations were of stone from the quarries of Prophetes Elias to the west of Delphi; the poros columns, six of which are now partly restored using the ancient material, were plastered; the temple was entered by a ramp, which was customary in Peloponnesian Temples. The partly preserved tiled floor of the pteron, pronaos and opisthodomos give an idea of the plan of the interior, as the walls have been robbed out for the lead of the clamps in their stones. On the north side an attempt at the restoration of the sekos has taken place and a column drum from the colonnade of the pteron has been put on the stylobate, on the three steps which form the krepis. The roof and pedimental reliefs were of Parian marble. According to Pausanias, the arrival of Apollo at Delphi was depicted on the east pediment, as also on that of the Alcmaeonid Temple, while on the west pediment Dionysos was portrayed with the Maenads (Thyiads). The metopes carried no sculptures but Persian shields were added to them after Marathon and Galatian after 279 BC. The Alcmaeonid sculptures, the omphalos, adyton, etc. are described below in the Museum section. The walls of the pronaos carried inscriptions on herms with the sayings of the seven sages of Greece such as "Know thyself" and "Nothing to Excess". The letter "E" was also inscribed and, when Plutarch was a priest at Delphi, he wrote a whole treatise on this, without making clear what it meant. There was also a bronze statue of Homer with the words of an oracle given to the blind poet on its base. The sekos was divided in two: in front was an altar to Poseidon, the forerunner of Apollo, statues of two Fates of Zeus Moiragetes and Apollo Moiragetes. There was also an iron throne, on which Pindar sat, when he came to Delphi and sang hymns to Apollo. The altar of Hestia in the pronaos was regarded as an altar for all the Greeks, it was here that the priests of Apollo killed Neoptolemos, the son of Achilles (see no. 74 above). The inner part of the sekos, the adyton, has been described above with the oracle and methods of prophesy. Pausanias says that very few had the right of entry to the adyton where, among other things, the gold statue of Apollo was placed. Kassotis, the prophetic fountain of Ge and the Muses, which had been incorporated into the temple in the archaic period, was moved, perhaps for safety, outside the temple to the north (see no. 66 above).

High above the temple, in the west part of the sanctuary are the spring of the older Kassotis (Kassotis I), the Shrine of the muses (**80**) and the remains of two unidentified archaic treasuries (**81-82**) with three more (**83-85**) lower down. North of the temple is the long retaining wall, the *Ischegaon* (ischo=to retain,ga=earth). Its name is mentioned in the inscriptions of the accounts for the rebuilding of the temple in the 4th century BC (after 356 BC). The bronze charioteer was found crushed by falling rocks behind the Ischegaon. A statue of some sort probably stood in a niche in the Ischegaon (marked on the plan).

Northwest of the temple going towards the theatre there are statue bases (**86-87**) on the left while to the right the famous Offering of Krateros (**88**) is set in a rectangular niche. A well-known scene from Alexander's march into Asia was shown here. According to the description of Plutarch, the general Krateros saved Alexander's life at a lionhunt near Susa in Persia. The general's son, also called

Reconstruction of the votive offering of Krateros (F. Courby).

The theatre.▶
Reconstruction of the theatre (H. Schleif).▶

Krateros, dedicated the offering after 320 BC. The bronze group was made by the great sculptors of the epoch, Lysippus and Leochares. The inscription, high on the wall of the niche, narrates this story, which was illustrated many times, the most famous example being that found in 1957 at Pella in Macedonia.

Through the nearby Gate C´ in the enclosure wall is the great Stoa of the Aetolians (**89-90**), identified by an inscription on the inner wall. It was built from the proceeds of booty taken at the victory of 279 BC over the Galatians. A colonnade on the façade supported the stoa roof and another further inside divided the building in two. In Roman times the east section of the stoa was adapted for baths. In front of the stoa are offering bases.

A magnificent stair leads to the theatre from the Krateros Offering. It was possibly never completed because, as it is now, it is a blind alley and the present ascent is by a road almost parallel to the ancient stair. The remains of an unidentified treasury (**91**) lie by this road.

The Theatre (**92**) has all the usual appointments of an ancient Greek theatre and is one of the better preserved. It was originally built in the 4th century BC of white stone from Parnassos and probably replaced an earlier one made of wood. The auditorium has 35 rows of seats divided by a gangway which was accessible from Gate E´ in the enclosure wall, the lower part and stage being reached by Gate D´. Eight stairways facilitated circulation in the lower part of the auditorium and divided it into seven tiers. The narrowness of the area above the gangway limits the tiers there to six, although a full semi-circle should have had double those below, ie. fourteen. The theatre was enlarged in the 2nd century BC with money and slaves sent by Eumenes II of Pergamon about 159 BC, according to an inscription. In the 1st century AD a marble frieze was added to the metopes of the skene (stage-building) representing the Labours of Heracles. It is on show in the Museum in the vestibule. The skene was in two parts with a proscenium in front divided in three parts corresponding to those in the building behind it. The skene was low so that the audience could enjoy the wonderful view. The orchestra, 18.50 m in diameter, was tiled and had a gutter for drainage all round it. The seating capacity is about 5000. At the big festivals the emphasis was on dramatic and lyrical performances. As the theatre was a much frequented place different decrees and acts, such as manumissions, are carved on its walls.

The east entrance (parodos) to the theatre leads to the remaining monuments of the sanctuary. These consist of two unidentified treasuries (**93-94**) and the remains of an archaic building, the Poteidanion (**95**).

THE STADIUM

A full tour of Delphi should include a visit to the stadium, although the path up from the theatre is steep and takes time. Halfway up the ancient spring of *Kerna* can be seen and the niches for offerings cut in the rock around it.

The first stadium was built in the 5th century BC, as can be ascertained from an inscription built into its south wall. Initially there were no seats for the audience and the seats of stone from Parnassos (not marble as Pausanias says) were paid for by Herodes Atticus in the time of Hadrian. Four bulky pillars in the entrance supported three arches; there were niches for statues in the two central ones. The beginning and end of the track are marked by two rows of oblong slabs with notches for the runners' feet at the start and with square holes for the posts which divided the competitors. The length was about 178 m (the Pythian stade was

The stadium from the east.

exactly 178.35 m, the Roman 177.55 m) and the width about 25.50 m. The two long sides of seats are united by the curved end of the stadium and are separated from the track by a small podium 1.30 m high, which is composed of a foundation course, upright blocks and katalepter (a course along the top). Circulation was facilitated by stairs at the east ends of the long sides and at the curved end and by others which divided the rows of seats, as well as a gangway all round above the seats. There are twelve rows of seats on the north side, where the landscape is suitable, and one with a backrest, and six rows on the south side; they accommodated about 7000 spectators. In the middle of the north side is a long bench with a backrest which replaces two rows of seats. This is the seat for the judges and other important people. There is a fountain with an arch above it at the northwest end for the thirsty audience. In 1971 fragments of Doric architectural pieces from a 6th century fountain, which had been there before the stadium, were found in its Roman debris.

THE MUSEUM

The Museum at Delphi houses one of the most important collections of original masterpieces of ancient Greek art.

The history of the exhibition in the present Museum building began in 1936, when the Greek archaeologial Service enlarged the building and the exhibits were re-organised with the help of the French archaeologist, Pierre de la Coste Messelière. At the end of 1939 the Second World War frustrated this work before the new exhibition could be opened to the public. On the Italian declaration of war on Greece on Oct. 28th 1940, the Museum at Delphi was dismantled, as were the other large Greek Museums. The exhibits were hidden in safe places such as caves and tombs or deeply buried. After the submission of Greece, the charioteer was taken secretly, to the National Archaeological Museum in Athens where, during the dark period of foreign occupation, his presence in the workshop encouraged young Greek archaeologists. In front of him the unforgettable Constantine A. Romaios and Christos Karouzos held unofficial, not to say secret, lectures. The new arrangement of exhibits in Greek museums only began after 1950. At Delphi, after the necessary repairs and some new building, the Ephor of Antiquities, Ioanna Konstantinou, gave a contemporary aspect to the exhibition. The recent Ephor, Petros Themelis, set up the display in the room with the chryselephantine objects and the silver bull, which was opened on July 26th 1978. He also began a new reorganisation in Rooms 9 and 11, which was only half-finished on his transfer to Athens.

Originally the exit was by the same stair which leads up to the Vestibule (1) but this caused congestion when visitors increased, so a second stair was constructed for the exit involving the division of the last Room into Rooms 13 and 1a, the latter now being accessible from the Vestibule (1).

The display is not completely in chronological order but most rooms cover a group of finds from a common find spot, such as those from the Apollo Temple, the Athenian Treasury, the Tholos of the Pronaia, etc. Almost all the rooms display unique objects.

The Vestibule (1)

A few unrelated important finds are displayed. First is the symbol of Delphi, the omphalos (navel-stone) (**8194**). The traveller Pausanias saw it in front of the Apollo Temple in the 2nd century AD and it was found there during modern excavation. This is a Hellenistic or early Roman copy of that in the adyton of the Apollo Temple. It is covered with an agrenon, that is the mesh of woollen fillets carved in relief which normally decorates an omphalos. On the original the knots were decorated with gorgon-shaped ornaments and above it were two gold eagles. As described above, in Classical times the omphalos symbolised the centre of the earth, since the two eagles Zeus freed at the ends of the world met here at Delphi. Also, however, the oval shape of the omphalos was reminiscent of a burial mound and, according to legend, hid the bones of the god Dionysos or the remains of the serpent, Pytho, which had been buried near the primitive oracle of its mother, Ge.

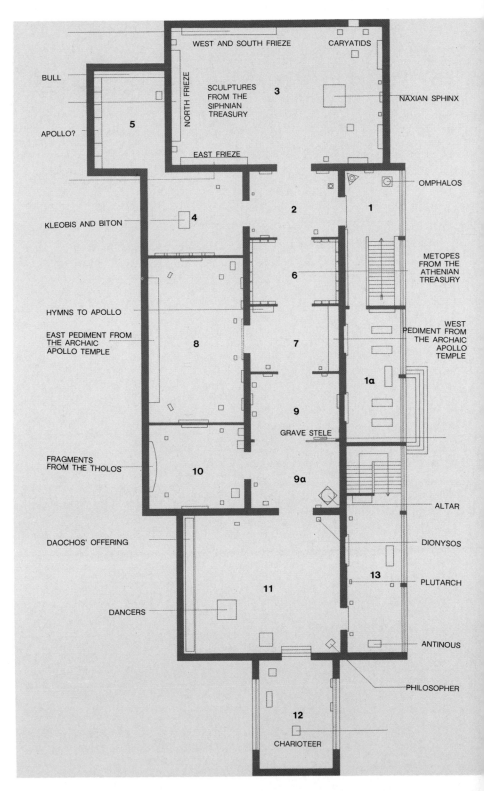

WEST AND SOUTH FRIEZE

CARYATIDS

BULL

NORTH FRIEZE

SCULPTURES
FROM THE
SIPHNIAN
TREASURY

3

NAXIAN SPHINX

APOLLO?

5

EAST FRIEZE

OMPHALOS

2

1

KLEOBIS AND BITON

4

METOPES
FROM THE
ATHENIAN
TREASURY

6

HYMNS TO APOLLO

EAST PEDIMENT FROM
THE ARCHAIC
APOLLO TEMPLE

8

7

WEST
PEDIMENT FROM
THE ARCHAIC
APOLLO
TEMPLE

1α

9

GRAVE STELE

FRAGMENTS
FROM THE THOLOS

10

9α

ALTAR

DAOCHOS' OFFERING

DIONYSOS

13

PLUTARCH

11

DANCERS

ANTINOUS

PHILOSOPHER

12

CHARIOTEER

Plan of the Museum.

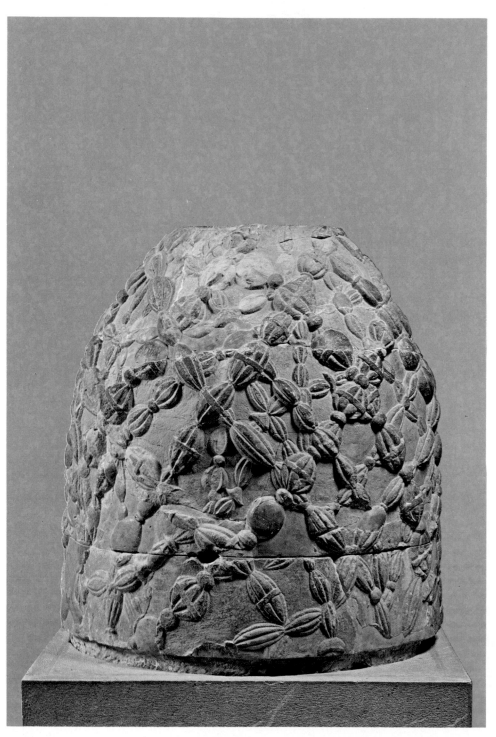

A marble omphalos (decorated with "agrinon").

Another symbolic object is the iron tripod (**9467**) with feet in the shape of a bull's hoof. It calls to mind the tripod in the temple adyton which supported a bowl for incense. There were many similar offerings in the Apollo Temple. The bowl in the Museum display, which has been put there to fill out the exhibition, does not belong to the tripod, as it is of a different date and style. A relief on a shelf against the wall shows Apollo and Athena right and left of the omphalos (**2707**). Below is a decree honouring the Athenian orator, Demades (about 330 BC), but only a few lines are preserved.

In the corridor to Room 1a, on the right leaning on the wall below, are the 1st century AD reliefs from the metopes of the skene (stage-house of the theatre). They depict the Labours of Heracles (**2544**) and show from left to right: 1) Heracles in the Garden of the Hesperides, 2) Cerberos, Heracles and the Nemean Lion, 3) Heracles wrestling with a Centaur, 4) Heracles overcoming the Lernaean Hydra, 5) Heracles wrestling with Antaios, 6) a scene of an Amazonomachy and Heracles, 7) Three-headed Geryon, 8) Heracles taming the horses of Diomedes, 9) Heracles against Diomedes, son of Ares and king of the Bistones in Thrace, 10) Heracles and the Stymphalian Birds.

The New Room 1a

This room is the east part of the former Room 13; it is now accessible from the Vestibule. It displays objects which were originally in Room 13, as well as new finds. Moving anti-clockwise:

Case 1. Top shelf: clay, bronze and gold ornaments and pots from tombs at Amphissa. Late 8th and 7th century BC. Middle shelf: Proto-Corinthian vases from Delphi, late 8th to mid 7th century BC; on the right Corinthian vases from Delphi, 7th century BC. Bottom shelf: Corinthian vases from Delphi, 7th century BC and, on the right, Proto-Corinthian and Corinthian vases from tombs at Amphissa. Late 8th to 6th century BC.

Case 2. Geometric vases from Delphi, 900-700 BC.

Case 3. (free standing). On the two upper shelves are bronze Geometric figurines of men, animals, birds, etc. from the Apollo Sanctuary, 900-700 BC, and below, parts of bronze Geometric tripods. 8th century BC.

Case 4. Attachments and other parts of bronze cauldrons and utensils in the shape of griffins, sirens, bovine heads, lions, boars, etc.

Case 5. Top shelf: a bronze statue of Apollo, 2nd quarter of 5th century BC; another of Dionysos or Apollo, 300-250 BC, and bronze figurines from Archaic to Hellenistic, 7th to 3rd century BC.

Middle shelf: bronze statuette of a youth, 430-420 BC, and another from Phthiotis of early Hellenistic date. Mythological scenes, such as Heracles showing the Erymantian Boar to Eurystheus, who is hiding in a pithos, or Odysseus, fleing from the Cyclops underneath a ram are represented on small bronzes. An eagle and other animals are also depicted.

Bottom shelf: bronze archaic figurine and other miniatures, such as the forequarters of dogs, human limbs, parts of legs, etc., 7th to 6th century BC.

Case 6. Attachments and other parts of bronze vessels and utensils, some of which come from Asia. Note, on the centre shelf, a bronze griffin and an embossed thunderbolt (the weapon of Zeus) and, on the bottom shelf, a bronze libation bowl with embossed scenes.

1. *Bronze statue of a youth.*
2. *Bronze siren from a lebes.*
3. *Odysseus tied beneath the ram.*

Case 7. Weapons and other bronze objects from the Apollo Sanctuary. Top shelf: bronze helmets. Middle shelf: decorated metal plates, buckles, pins of different types and an inscription ARCHIPPA ELYTHIA on a circular metal plate.

Bottom shelf: weapon points, axes, etc.

Case 8. Clay vases and figurines from a sanctuary at Kirrha, the port of Delphi. Note a spouted kylix, closed above. It has black figure decoration on a white ground in its upper register, and red-figure decoration between the handles.

The Room of the Shields (2)

Three bronze shields are hung on the walls. The first from the right (**7226**) is decorated with embossed concentric circles cut by two V shaped lines. This type is known by a north European name, Herzsprung, where the first example was found. Since then similar shields have come to light on Greek land (Cyprus, Rhodes, Crete) and also in the Iberian Peninsula, Ireland and elsewhere in north Europe, where U shaped lines appear instead of V shaped ones. This example belongs to the first half of the 7th century BC and was an offering in the Sanctuary of Apollo. The other two shields (**7227, 7177**) are decorated with an embossed lion

1. Bronze griffin head.
2. Bronze "daedalic" statuette.

protome with other animals incised round it, such as lions, rams, deer, etc. On one of them two figures can be seen between the lion's feet. Many shields of this type come from the Idaean Cave on Crete and belong to about 700 BC. They are similar to an Assyrian type of shield of the 10th and even more to one of the 9th century BC.

On the right and left of the entrance to Room 4 are two griffin protomes, that on the left (**7734**) is of hammered bronze, while that on the right (**8396**) is bronze cast. They were attached to the shoulders of bronze bowls and are similar to many others, especially those found at Olympia.

On the left a small bronze kouros (**2527**) 19 cms high possibly represents Apollo. It is thought to be Cretan work from the mid-Daedalic period, ie. second half of 7th century BC.

Immediately to the right of the entrance to this room is the marble pedestal of a sprinkler (**5733**), composed of three korai. It is restored with plaster and belongs to the first quarter of the 6th century BC. There are better preserved and more well-known examples from Corinth, in the Poseidon Temple at Isthmia (now in the new museum at Kyra Brysi) and from Sparta. They were used for a ritual cleansing of hands at shrines, as is still the practice today in Catholic churches.

The Room of the Siphnian Treasury (3)

This room, the largest in the Museum, contains a very important collection for the history of archaic Greek sculpture. It consists of unique Ionic pieces from the Aegean islands.

In the centre of the right side is the famous Naxian Sphinx, dedicated by this island in the Apollo Sanctuary about 560 BC (site plan no. 41). At this time Naxos was at the height of its prosperity and even tried to control the sacred island of Delos, where she dedicated a smaller marble sphinx. The exotic Naxian Sphinx, with its unique carving, dominated the Sanctuary, rising on an Ionic base 12.10 m high. The Sphinx itself is 2.32 m high, so the height of the whole offering was more than 14.40 m. It has a woman's head, like an archaic kore with characteristic smile, a bird's breast and wings and a lion's body and feet. The details were emphasised with colour. Mythical representations of monsters came to Greece from Asia, but the delicacy of the representations and the harmonious combination of the different parts smoothly changing from animal and monster to human, such as this sphinx head, is characteristic of the Greek spirit. The Sphinx, the emblem of Naxos, was set on the site of the ancient shrine of Ge (which had been guarded by the Pytho, whom Apollo killed) because it was one of Ge's demons and so would guard the shrine as once the Pytho had. At the base of the offering, on the lowest column drum with its 44 shallow flutes, a Delphian decree was carved renewing the right of promanteia to Naxos in 328-327 BC.

The sculptures from the Siphnian Treasury are very well preserved and take up most of the room. Herodotus (3.57) says that the Siphnians built one of the richest treasuries at Delphi (site plan no. 19). It must have been finished by 525 BC when Samian refugees plundered the island, putting an end to its prosperity. The frieze sculptures seem to have been executed by at least two artists. The craftsman who made the carvings on the south and west sides of the treasury was more conservative in his art, as it is faithful to the Ionic tradition from the shores of Asia Minor, while the one who worked on the east and north sides facing the Sacred Way, seems more ingenious, being influenced by a training in Chian workshops and, even more, by Athenian technique. All the sculptures were picked out in bright colours of which traces are preserved; the ground was blue and traces of red and green on clothes and hair and on the warrior's shields are still present. Many of the weapons had portions in inlaid bronze and many of the figures had their names painted on them.

The East Frieze depicts the Trojan War (right) watched by the gods of Olympos (left). The seated gods are divided into Greek and Trojan supporters. On the left are those friendly to Troy: Ares in armour by himself at the end, Aphrodite (or Leto) talking with Artemis and Apollo, while Zeus (head missing) is seated on a magnificent throne decorated with a satyr chasing a nymph. On his right are the Greek supporters: at his feet Thetis, mother of Achilles, is shown, perhaps kneeling, as she prays to the almighty father of the gods. This section is missing except for parts of fingers resting on Zeus' knees. To the right were shown Poseidon (missing), Athena, Hera and Demeter (or Hebe). In the right portion of this side the battle unfolds: a four horse chariot driven by Glaucos belongs to the Trojans; next Aeneas and Hector fight against Menelaus (with a gorgonhead on his shield) and Ajax over the body of a dead warrior. The fourhorse chariot on the right is Greek and driven by Automedon. Nestor, an able warrior and orator, stands in front of it, encouraging the Greeks with his raised right hand.

The Sphinx from Naxos.

1. *Treasury of the Siphnians: Ares, Aphrodite, Artemis, Apollo, Zeus.*
2. *Greeks and Trojans from the east frieze of the Siphnian treasury.*

The North Frieze shows the Gigantomachy, that is the war of the gods of Olympos against the Giants. On the left, Hephaistos at his forge fills his bellows with air to prepare red-hot iron missiles. In front of him two goddesses fight two Giants. Further on Cybele is shown in a chariot drawn by two impressive lions, which are lacerating a Giant while behind her Heracles armed with his lionclub fights another. On the right Apollo and Artemis aim arrows at three Giants while, between them at the back, the Giant Kantharos runs fearfully towards the right looking behind him. His emblem is on the crest of his helmet, ie. the vase called a kantharos. Further on Zeus was shown in his chariot (not preserved) fighting two Giants; his wife Hera bends over a Giant she has thrown to the ground. Further to the right Athena fights the Giant Laertes; another Giant has already fallen to the

1. *Gods and giants from the north frieze of the Siphnian treasury.*
2. *Gods and giants from the north frieze of the Siphnian treasury.*

ground. Next, Ares fights two Giants, Viatos and Enaphos, and Hermes fights two others with his spear. On the right end Poseidon can be seen (restored in plaster), and perhaps Amphitrite, fighting two Giants. The sculptor wrote his name on the third of the Giants fighting Apollo and Artemis, but this part of the inscription is worn and the wonderful craftsman remains unknown.

The West Frieze which was on the façade, pictures the Judgement of Paris. According to the myth, Eris, Goddess of Discord, was not invited to the wedding of Peleus and Thetis and, to avenge herself, she threw an apple among the guests inscribed "to the most beautiful". This caused trouble between Hera, Athena and Aphrodite. Zeus appointed Paris as judge and he gave the apple to Aphrodite. On

1. Section of the Gigantomachy from the north frieze of the Siphnian treasury.
2. Four-horse chariot in front of an altar, from the south frieze of the Siphnian treasury.

the frieze the story is shown in three parts, one for each goddess: on the left a winged Athena ascends her chariot drawn by winged horses driven by Hermes. A god behind her is perhaps Hephaistos or Poseidon. In the centre of the frieze the winner, Aphrodite, descends from her chariot, coquetishly fingering her necklace. She is the most beautiful figure of the whole Siphnian frieze. The third part on the right is not preserved but it must have shown Hera with her chariot.

The South Frieze is known from a few fragments but they are insufficient to reveal the theme. One of the pieces shows the abduction of a female figure by an unidentified hero, who is mounting a chariot (Pelops and Hippodameia or the

1. Karyatid from the façade of the treasury of the Siphnians.
2. Head of a Karyatid from the treasury of the Siphnians.

Dioscuri with the daughters of Leucippus). Another chariot is shown in front of an altar and part of a third and two horses are also present.

On the right and left of the Naxian Sphinx the remains of the two caryatids, who supported te entablature of the Siphnian Treasury façade instead of columns, are displayed. The better preserved on the left retains most of her body and her head with a polos, on which was a capital decorated with two lions tearing a deer to pieces (displayed on a separate base on the left). The full height of the column would be made up by the missing lower body and high base. Holes in the hair and diadem show that they were once decorated with metal ornaments. The caryatid is wearing a thin chiton with a wide himation above it, which falls in deep folds.

Silenoi and Maenads are shown in relief on the polos (or basket). The head on the right of the Sphinx wears a cylindrical polos depicting Apollo in relief playing a lyre, with four nymphs next to him and the Three Graces in front of him together with Hermes playing the pipe. This head was originally attributed to the Cnidian or another Ionic treasury. There are, indeed, noteworthy differences between the two heads, not only of craftsmanship but also in the shape of the face, in the eyes, which, in the second head, were of inlaid stones and slanting upwards, in the intense smile, etc.

In antiquity the ornate entrance to the sekos would have been seen between the caryatids at the back of the pronaos. Its remains, partly restored, are on the wall behind the better preserved Caryatid. It was decorated with relief rosettes, lotus and other flowers, similarly to the better preserved entrance to the Erechtheion on the Acropolis in Athens. Indeed the Siphnian caryatids are forerunners of those of the Erechtheion.

Right and left of the entrance are important exhibits unrelated to the Siphnian Treasury. They belong to a construction, which covered an honoured offering or religious object in the archaic Apollo Temple (last quarter of 6th century BC) and were decorated with Ionic moulding, knucklebones, anthemia, lotus flowers, etc. The Aeolic capital comes from the Massaliote Treasury in the Pronaia Sanctuary and also belongs to the archaic period (530-510 BC) along with other objects in the room.

The East Pediment (Nothing from the relief decoration of the West Pediment has been found). The sculptures of the east pediment are fairly well preserved, the height at the centre being 0.73 m. This pediment is unusual as the lower parts are in relief while the upper portions are in the round. The theme is the well-known one

Herakles' attempt to steal the tripod; east pediment of the Siphnian treasury.

of the struggle between Heracles and Apollo for the Delphic tripod. It is also depicted on vase painting and other works of art. The myth relates that Heracles, in a rage because the Pythia refused him an oracle, as he had not been cleansed of the murder of Iphitus, seized the prophetic tripod intending to found his own oracle. On the pediment the two gods are portrayed dragging the tripod, Heracles to the right, Apollo to the left, while in the middle a higher godlike figure, formerly interpreted as Athena or Zeus and now as Hermes, tries to separate the two quarrellers. Behind Apollo his sister Artemis (or his mother Leto) hold him back. Further to the left two female figures stand in front of a horse-drawn chariot whose charioteer is kneeling in the left corner, corresponding to the right end of the pediment where another chariot is shown after two figures, etc. Finally next to the Gigantomachy frieze high on the wall are parts of the Siphnian Treasury roof. On the left is a piece decorated with relief anthemia and lotus flowers and on the right a piece with a lionhead in the centre which was used as a water spout on the roof.

The Room of the Kouroi (4)

In contrast to the Ionic art of the Aegean islands in Room 3, Room 4 displays Doric art from the Peloponnese. Set a little back from the centre of the room are two splendid archaic marble kouroi. Many kouroi and korai are preserved in Greek Museums and in large foreign ones, such as the Metropolitan Museum, etc., but few are equal in size, artistic merit and historical interest to these two youths. The inscription gives their names as Kleobis and Biton and the artist "[Poly]medes of Argos made them". The legend is preserved in Herodotus (1.31): the Athenian, Solon, one of the seven sages of Greece, was being entertained in Sardis by

Bronze Kouros - possibly representing Apollo.

Archaic Kouroi: Kleobis and Biton. ▶

Croesus of Lydia. He was shown the huge wealth of the Lydian king and later Croesus asked him whom he thought was the richest and happiest person in the world, expecting to hear his own name in reply. Solon, however, named the Athenian, Tellos, and explained that Tellos had lived in a happy city, had children and beautiful grandchildren and died renowned and honoured. Then Croesus asked who came next and waited again to hear his name, but Solon mentioned Kleobis and Biton. They were well-endowed both in riches and in physique Argives, who had both won crowns in the games. At the time of the festival of Hera their mother, who was one of Hera's priestesses, had to go from Argos to the Heraion, but there was a delay in bringing the oxen from the meadow and, since time was passing, the two sons took the oxens' place in the wagon and brought their mother to the Heraion about 8 kilometers away. They were highly praised and their mother prayed to Hera to reward her sons with whatever was best, with the result that they went happily to sleep that day and never woke up again. The Argives dedicated their statues at Delphi as being the ''best of mortals'',as Herodotus said. The statues are 2.16 m high and are two of the oldest kouroi, dating to about 600 BC, when Daedalic art was developing into early Archaic. Earlier art historians attributed a lack of life to the archaic kouroi and korai. Closer study has revealed that the slight movement of the whole body is reflected in the arrangement of every hair, muscle, etc., a phenomenon common in archaic art.

Today there are few who do not acknowledge the qualities of this art. Kleobis and Biton do not have the motion of a discus thrower, but this was not the artist's intention. He wished to continue a tradition and he succeeds in his own fashion. Although the archaic kouroi do not move as discus-throwers, yet they give an impression of hidden strength.

The statues of Kleobis and Biton were found in pieces behind the Athenian Treasury in 1893 and later: one of the two plinths was found by A. Keramopoullos in 1934, built into the baths by the Roman Agora. Recently, however, the identity of the statues has been disputed; some people see them as the Dioscuri, who were especially worshipped in Laconia.

In the righthand part of the room in a special case is a small bronze kouros (**1663**) perhaps representing Apollo. He is naked apart from sandals and a necklace. His hair, confined on his head in a net, falls in beautiful waves onto his chest. He is considered a good example of Laconian art for the period 550-540 BC or a little earlier.

On the left wall are the metopes of the poros monopteral, the Sicyonian Treasury (site plan no. 16), dating to about 560 BC. They are unusually long (88 by 58 cms). Only five of the fourteen metopes survive and they are not on the whole well preserved but traces of colour survive and some details have been incised.

The first metope on the left depicts the expedition of the Argonauts. The prow of their swift boat, Argo, appears with the shields which protect the sailors fixed over the gunwale. Orpheus and someone beside him play the lyre to calm the waves. On the right and left the metopes are framed by two riders facing forwards, the Dioscuri, Castor and Polydeuces, who are said to have disembarked on horseback. The artist shows marvellous ability in his synthesis, daring and craftsmanship, which enables him to present so clear a picture in so small an area.

The second metope shows the Rape of Europa by Zeus, changed into a bull. According to the myth, Europa, a Phoenician princess, was loved by Zeus, who changed himself into a beautiful bull on which she rode to Crete, where she gave birth to the two judges of Hades, Minos and Rhadamanthys. On the metope

1. Metope from the monopteral treasury of the Sikyonians.
2. Wild boar on a metope from the monopteral treasury of the Sikyonians.

Europa is bending forward clasping the bull round the neck; her attitude expresses the swift forward motion of the bull.

The third metope is the best preserved. Castor and Polydeuces armed with spears in both hands are depicted with their cousins Idas and Lynkeus, children of Apharidas, in a variation of the myth given by Pindar (*Nem.* 60ff) according to which they stole oxen in Arcadia. The ceremonial arrangement of the composition is noteworthy. The names of the heroes (Lynkeus is missing) are incised and high-lighted with paint.

The fourth metope portrays a stage in the story of the Caledonian Boar who ravaged Aetolia. Meleager's dog, who finally killed the boar, can be seen below it.

The fifth metope presents the theft fo the Golden Fleece which Phrixos stole riding a ram.

The Room of the Bull (5)

The excavation of the Apollo Temple had for long been considered almost finished when, in 1939, the present Director of the French School of Archaeology, Professor P. Amandry, then a young archaeologist and secretary of the School, found a treasure hidden under the pavement of the Sacred Way. The aim of the excavation had been to study the tiles but below the pavement, in front of the Athenian Treasury and in the area of the Halos, were found two dumping grounds for sacred objects at a depth of only 20 cms. They were full of gold, ivory, silver, bronze, iron and clay fragments mixed with earth, carbon and ash. All these finds came up in a single week, but their importance was realised later, when the fragments were cleaned and put together by the Greek Museum technicians (G. Bakoulis and A. Mavraganis). The largest dump contained the richest finds. They included parts of three unique, lifesize, chryselephantine statues. A wonderful surprise came when tiny, smashed pieces of silver from the second dump made up into a bull. The sacred debris had been buried in the dumps in the mid-5th century BC after a fire burnt the building where they were stored. Many are works of Ionic art, some perhaps coming from Asia Minor. Their display in this new room is the work of the Ephor of Antiquities, P. Themelis.

Proceeding from right to left:

Case 1. Numbered in the following series are: 1) a bronze statuette of a flute player, a fine early 5th century BC piece; 2) part of a bone flute; 3) on a single base an athlete, with dumbells and a crown, and a judge. An Attic piece of bronze-casting 460-450 BC; 4) an ivory group of two sphinxes with a single head, a marvellous 6th century piece; 5-6) two pairs of bronze sphinxes facing each other on an Ionic capital; 7-8) parts of bronze sheet cutouts with embossed and incised decoration, 6th century BC; 9) a silver kylix on a high foot; 10) the ivory lower jaw of a horse; 11) a gold plated silver libation bowl and a bronze one.

Case 2. 1) An ivory statuette of a god who holds a spear in his right hand, while leaning the left on the head of a lion or panther reared up on its hind legs. It is one of the oldest exhibits in the room and is an Ionic piece with eastern influence. The male god corresponds to a female goddess called the potnia theron - the lady of the animals. Early 7th century BC; 2-3) two bronze sirens with bird bodies and female heads which were cauldron handles. Of eastern origin, late 8th century BC; 4) two gold plates in the shape of a kylix with an eye, perhaps for sheathing a small

1. Bronze statuette of a pipe-player.
2. Ivory statuette of a god.

wooden Ionic capital; 5) an inscribed bronze base from a censer of eastern origin; 6) bronze tips attached to spear butts to enable them to stand in the ground; 7) bronze or iron arrow tips.

Case 3. Different pieces from a chryselephantine statue of a god, probably Apollo, sitting on a throne. An Ionic piece, 6th century BC. 1) The partly restored ivory head of the god with hair made from a plate of beaten gold with two gold tresses falling onto his chest; 2) in his right hand the god held a silver plated libation bowl; 3) two gold plates with eight embossed animal representations fringing the god's clothing, which was richly decorated; 4) his ivory feet, which protruded under his clothing; 5) above left: his gold diadem with six applied rosettes; 6) below: gold plates attached to bronze plaques with embossed decoration (griffin, two gorgons, three rosettes) are part of the decoration of his throne; 7) above right: gold tresses belong to the back of the god's head; 8) gold lionheads from a necklace; 9) ivory bands with applied gold rosettes; 10) gold plates with embossed decoration belonging to clothing; 11) pieces of ivory from the god's hand.

Case 4. Different pieces of similar chryselephantine female statues of the

Head, probably of Apollo, made of ivory, silver and gold.

same date and of similar outstanding craftsmanship, perhaps Apollo's sister, the goddess Artemis, and their mother Leto. 1) An ivory female head with a gold diadem and gold rosette earrings; 2) two attached pieces of an ivory hand wearing a gold bracelet and holding a sceptre; 3) gold tresses of hair; 4) a gold diadem; 5) a less well preserved ivory head thought to belong to Leto; 6) gold bracelets and anklets; 7) ivory toes perhaps belonging to the goddess; 8) two more ivory pairs of feet with exquisite sandals which must belong to smaller female figures.

Case 5. A variety of small pieces in different materials. 1) Gold and bronze leaves; 2) three clay female figurines; 3) parts of applied decoration from furniture, ie. ivory cut out plaques, heads, hands and bare feet, 6th century BC; 4) three similar ivory heads from chryselephantine statuettes; 5-6) heads and hands from

Gold and ivory head, probably of Artemis.

ivory statuettes, 6th century BC; 7) a gold diadem; 8) pieces from ivory groups with cutout figures in relief; a group representing the Harpies, Aello and Okypede, running to the right after snatching Phineas' food, while the winds, Zetes and Kalais, chase them; above at a small table a hand can be seen which is thought to be that of Phineas. This piece is a miracle of Corinthian miniature art, about 570 BC; 9-10) partly preserved ivory groups representing the battles of the Trojan War are similar pieces. They come from the decoration of small boxes.

Case 6. Similar miniatures some of especial interest. 1) Ivory cutout plaques, heads, hands and feet; 2) ivory decorative plaques ornamented with meanders and rosettes; 3) fragments of two ivory bulls facing each other, 6th century BC; 4) below: the Chimaera, a mythical beast with a lionhead, a tail ending in a dragon-

Bronze incence-burner.
◄*The head of the silver bull.*

head and a goat's protome above the centre of the body. Gold decorative bands and flowers; 5) a group of ivory cutout figures in relief portraying the departure of a warrior in a fourhorse chariot, perharps Amphiaraos, Ionic miniature, 6th century BC; 6-7) ivory groups of similar craftsmanship representing warriors; 8-9) two gold flowers; 10) small bronze shields and vase handles; 11) iron spear points. A large case the length of the back wall contains the lifesize silver bull (**10660**). Its original dimensions were about 2.30 by 1.25 m. It was made of hammered silver sheets held together by bronze bands and attached to a wooden core with silver nails. It is a wonderful example of 6th century Ionic art. It was destroyed in the second half of the 5th century BC, piously buried in the dump near the Halos, with the other objects in this room, under the paving of the Sacred Way and found in 1939 in an unrecognisable condition. Its present restoration is the work of technicians from the National Archaeological Museum, Athens.

A bronze censer, which is held above her head by a female figure wearing a peplos, is exhibited on a special stand. The censer is shaped like a hemi-spherical cauldron; incense was put in it and covered by a perforated lid. Wonderful workmanship, probably from the island of Paros, about 450 BC.

Theseus and an Amazon, on a metope from the treasury of the Athenians.

Herakles killing the Kerynian stag; metope from the treasury of the Athenians. ▶

The Room of the Athenian Treasury (6)

This room contains the 24 better preserved metopes from the Treasury of the Athenians (site plan no. 30). There were thirty in all, six on the short sides and nine on the long. Those from the façade showed scenes from the Amazonomachy. The theme of those of the north and west sides is the frequent one of the Labours of Heracles, while that of the south side, which was seen from the Sacred Way, was reserved for the Labours of Theseus, the preeminent Athenian hero, who founded Athens with the people already living in Attica. The representations on each metope are described on the Museum labels. There were five or six craftsmen varying from the more conservative to those who opened the road from the Late Archaic period to the Early Classical period of Attic art.

In the same room are a few remains from the pedimental sculptures of the treasury. The two most important Greek heroes seem to have been shown: Theseus and Heracles. On the east pediment a peaceful meeting of two heroes is depicted: Theseus and Perithous, king of the Lapiths, in front of a goddess. On the west pediment was a battle scene with Heracles as its chief figure; with a fellow warrior, Telamon of Salamis, he fights the king of Troy, Laomedon, father of Priam.

Immediately right of the entrance are parts of Hymns to Apollo, which were carved in 128 BC on the south wall of the treasury with notes for singing in the upper part and for the instrumental music below. The notes have been deciphered by the Germans, Fr. Bellermann and K. Fortlage.

The Rooms of the Apollo Temple (7-8)

The chief pieces preserved from the Archaic temple of the Alcmaeonids are the pedimental sculptures. The pieces on the right of the entrance to Room 7 come from the west poros pediment, which displayed the Gigantomachy. There are bits of Athena attacking a kneeling Giant, parts of the chests of two horses, etc. (the visitor should consult the reconstructed plan). The famous Athenian sculptor, Antenor, is thought to have carved it and the surviving pieces are certainly worthy of his skill.

Next to the pediment is a small headless marble kouros, about 500 BC, and beyond him a goddess wearing a peplos, identified hypothetically as Iris or Nike. It could have been the akroterion of the so-called Doric Treasury in the Pronaia Sanctuary. It belongs to the decade 480-470 BC. In the big room on the right (8) are displayed parts of the marble pediment from the east end of the Apollo Temple. Its theme is the appearance of the god Apollo at Delphi, accompanied, as is shown, by his mother, Leto, and sister, Artemis. The god is shown in a fourhorse chariot which is facing frontwards, occupying the centre of the pediment. Corresponding figures are depicted right and left: on the right is Delphos, who, it is conjectured, as master of the site, received the god and two other figures, while on the left three female figures are thought to be the daughters of Cecrops, king of Athens, Pandrosos, Erse and Aglauros. The two corners of the pediment are each filled by a lion; that on the right mauls a deer that on the left throws down a bull. There are traces of red on the lion's mane, the blood from the wounds and the fringes of the clothes; other details must also have been emphasised in colour. To

Winged Victory, an akroterion from the temple of the Alkmeonidai.

the right of the pediment the central akroterion of the temple is displayed, a marble winged Nike, and near it, on a wall shelf, is part of the temple gutter, which ends in a lionhead spout. On the left side of the pediment, the side akroterion of the temple, a headless sphinx, is displayed and a gutter from the 4th century BC temple.

One of the statuettes of a youth belongs to the years 555-540 BC, the other to 540-520 BC. The bronze cow statuette, an offering to Apollo, is dated to about 500 BC. Two possible offerings from Paros are: 1) a stele of the mid-6th century BC of Parian marble (**997** and **3427**), an offering from the sons of Charopinos, who also dedicated the following exhibit; 2) a kouros of which only the base is saved. On the wall opposite the pediment the most important inscriptions for the history of the Apollo Temple are displayed. They consist of four stelai dating to the years 361-310 BC. The bills are written for the rebuilding of the temple after the fire of 373 BC and include a catalogue of the cities and private individuals, who gave money, and the amounts the Phocians had to pay after the Third Sacred War. Above the entrance to the room is an inscription in large letters mentioning repairs to the Apollo Temple under the emperor Domitian, 84 AD.

Grave relief of an athlete.

Marble altar from the temple of Pronaia.▶

The Room of the Funeral Monuments and the Altar (9-9a)

Until recently this room was divided by a partition which cut off the view to Room 12 and the charioteer. Now (1981) the partition has been moved to the left and is only used as a background to the exhibits and the room has recovered its unity, while the exhibits form two separate groups. In the first part (9) the grave stelai are kept.

Moving anti-clockwise from the entrance, part of a grave stele is displayed (**936**) of a man wearing a heavy himation, end of 6th century BC. A cremation urn follows belonging to a grave found in front of the Museum, 5th century BC. The following three clay female protomes (Demeter or Kore) came from a dump in front of the Museum, also 5th century BC. The bronze cremation urn in the next case comes from a grave in the village of Makrakomi in Phthiotis, first half of 4th century BC.

In the left half of the room a grave stele from the east cemetery at Delphi stands out for the quality of its workmanship: a young athlete scrapes himself with a strigil after a wrestling match. Unfortunately the head and lower legs are lost. In front of

him a slave stands holding an aryballos (probably for oil) in his right hand, while a dog's head is preserved between them, doubtless the youth's pet. Ionic or Boeotian workshop, mid-5th century BC.

In a case against the left wall different vases from 5th century BC graves can be seen. Against the wall left of the entrance a grave stele of a young slave-girl holding a mirror is placed. Mid-5th century BC.

In the second half of the room (9a) the visitor returns to the world of the gods and their temples. Moving anti-clockwise the statue of a running woman from the Pronaia Sanctuary is displayed, 4th century BC. Further on a headless marble statue is the usual early Hellenistic representation of Apollo playing the lyre (**1876**), early 3rd century BC. On the left against the wall is a relief protome of a horse from a fourhorse chariot. Part of a metope, end of 5th century BC.

The circular marble altar (8), 1.076 m high, was found in scattered pieces in the Pronaia Sanctuary. On the frieze six pairs of girls hang garlands. It is thought to have been placed in the Tholos or in the open air for the worship of divinities of the earth. 2nd century BC.

The Room of the Tholos (10)

Part of the reconstructed circular building in the Pronaia Sanctuary is on show here together with preserved architectural fragments with relief decoration. The chief sculptured decoration of the Tholos consists of two Doric friezes, one larger than the other, both made from Parian marble. The larger one was on the outside above the colonnade and epistyles, as was usual (this can be better appreciated from the restored portions of the Tholos on the site). The metopes are 65 by 62,50 cms and are 7cms thick and portray scenes from the Amazonomachy. Four of them can be seen partly restored. In the first on the left a centaur grabs a woman; in the second a horse with a naked rider is rearing up on its hind legs; in the third a naked Greek is attacked by an Amazon; in the fourth a man goes towards a dedication monument, where a female figure is standing, but the relief has been defaced.

On the shelves to the right and left parts of metopes from the large frieze are displayed and also some from the smaller frieze showing the Battle of the Centaurs. The smaller metopes were 42 by 40.5 cms and were 4 cms thick. They decorated the upper part of the sekos wall outside the Tholos and depicted the Labours of the two great mythical Greek heroes, Theseus and Heracles.

On special bases to the right and left parts of the akroterion of the Tholos, a Nike, are displayed and pieces of other akroteria.

The Tholos sculptures date to about 380 BC. Sculpted in high relief they are of first rate craftsmanship and portray the characteristic daring and free movement with tense, dramatic action combined with a grace of line. These sculptures leave behind the 5th century BC Polykleitian art and move into the 4th century Lysippian. The Roman architect, Vitruvius, mentions Theodore of Phocaia as the architect. The french archaeologist J. Marcadé noted the similarities between these sculptures and those of the Temple of Asclepius at Epidauros and maintains that Theodore must be the same person as he who is mentioned on the building inscriptions in the Temple of Asclepius.

The Room of the Daochos Offering (11)

This room is beyond Room 9a. There have been recent changes here as the result of a new arrangement of the Daochos monument by P. Themelis.

Moving anti-clockwise the statue of an athlete, 4th century BC, which used to be in Room 9, has been put immediately right of the entrance. It has been moved because it is identified as Telemachos and belongs to the Daochos Monument, which is next to it. Daochos II of Pharsala was tetrarch of Thessaly 337-332 BC, hieromnemon of Thessaly in the Amphictyonic League of Delphi and Chairman of

Sisyphos I, father of Daochos II.
The pankratiast, Agias.

the League. His monument stood in the Apollo Sanctuary (site plan no. 70). Inscriptions on the base, some in verse, laud the political, athletic and military achievements of members of this Thessalian family. The positions of nine marble statues can be seen on the base: Daochos, his son, six ancestors and the god Apollo, whose statue is unfortunately not preserved. Recent research has shown that he must have been seated on a rock or on the omphalos, as he is portrayed on coins of Delphi. He was at the right end of the line, as the recent arrangement shows, followed by the ancestors: Aknonios, dressed, three naked athletes: the pankratiast Agias, the wrestler Telemachos and the runner Agelaos; Daochos I and Sisyphos I both dressed and then Daochos II himself, also dressed, followed by his son, Sisyphos II, who is leaning on a stele. Only the plinth of the statue of the donor is left and the first athlete met on entering the room is Telemachos.

In the same half of the room the lower drum and upper part of the Acanthus Column with its dancers can be seen (site plan no. 72). The three dancers are

The "dancing girls" from the column with the acanthus.

◄Marble portrait of an aged philosopher.

◄Dionysos, from the west pediment of the temple.

wearing a transparent, high-girdled, short himation reaching to their knees. They are more than two metres high and stand on a peculiar acanthus capital. They hold their chitons with their lowered left hands, while the right are raised in the movement of the dance. On their heads they wear a basket-like polos. They supported a bronze tripod cauldron, which is standing on the projecting acanthus leaves. The total height was about 13m. It must have stood out not only for its height but also on account of its exotic appearance and its craftsmanship. It was set up after the catastrophic earthquake 373 BC. The base inscription shows it was an Athenian offering 332-322 BC.

Two more exhibits are now (1981) in the left part of the room: a marble portrait of an old man, perhaps a philosopher, (**1819**) 280-270 BC and a statue of Dionysos, from the west pediment of the 4th century BC temple.

The Room of the Charioteer (12)

To get the right impression of the unique charioteer the visitor should try to find the place from which the statue is best seen, that is a little further in from the centre of the entrance: an ancient statue can be looked at from several sides but there is only one primary view. Although this statue has suffered much during the centuries, yet its general preservation is good, apart from the loss of some of the coloured material decorating his diadem. Nothing has been restored.

The charioteer is one of the most famous examples of 5th century Greek art. He was part of a group dedicated by the Deinomenid tyrants of Syracuse, who also offered the gold tripods in the Apollo Sanctuary (site plan no. 65), after their victory over the Carthaginians at Himera. They are also known from the poems of Pindar and Bacchylides who praised their victories at the panhellenic games. The charioteer is the result of a victory in the chariot race at the Pythian Games of 478 or 474 BC by one of Deinomenes' sons, Polyzalos, tyrant of Gela, a patron of the arts. The partly preserved inscription on the base reads "Polyzalos dedicated me. Bless him, o Honoured Apollo". Part of the base can be seen in the right hand corner of the room. The group consisted of a fourhorse chariot, its driver and perhaps a groom, who drove the victor off the racecourse. The chariot hid the charioteer's lower body which accounts for its length. His left arm is missing. Other pieces of the group have been found: parts of three horses'legs, fragments of the pole and axle of the vehicle, parts of the reins and the right hand of a child, perhaps the groom. Some are on show on the right and left of the charioteer.

The charioteer is wearing a long, priestly chiton, customary for those taking part in sacred rites, as all the games the great festivals had a sacred character. The chiton is high-girdled with two bands which are gathered behind. The rich folds at the breast are in contrast to the fluted pleats below the girdle. The same antithesis is apparent in the lively curls on the cheeks in contrast to the simple but carefully contrived movement of the curls on the head, which seem almost glued on. The diadem is a sign of victory. The slight turn and inclination of the head and the shape of the face, with its flat cheeks in contrast to the intentionally full and asymmetrical chin and to the fleshy lips, are embellished by the "Greek profile" and crowned by the charioteer's gaze. Luckily the eyes are preserved untouched; they are made of white enamel with a black stone for the pupil, and are framed by the eyelashes and the slightly slanting eyebrows. The statue, with its portrayal of Olympian calm, is incomparable. The artist is unknown. The foremost ones of the

The Charioteer.

Detail of the Charioteer.
Apollo: painting on the inside of a kylix.▶

age were the Samian Pythagoras, and the somewhat younger Kalamis, who worked in Athens and made chariot races, but none of their work survives for comparison. The charioteer is a lucky find which gives an idea of the achievements of classical sculpture. He was covered for centuries by rocks, which fell in the earthquake of 373 BC, and came to light again during the French excavations in 1896 in a place between the Theatre, the Krateros Offering and the Ischegaon.

Against the wall to the left of the entrance the white-ground kylix is displayed (**8140**). It is decorated with a unique representation of Apollo. It is of the same period as the Charioteer 480-470 BC and is shown in the same room as an example of similar austere art. The painter drew Apollo with fine brown lines seated on a folding stool with its legs ending in lion's paws. He wears a sleeveless chiton fastened on the shoulders, while his back and lower body are wrapped in a purple himation; his hair is golden and his crown of myrtle leaves. With his right hand he pours a libation of wine from a libation bowl and with his left he strikes the strings of a seven-chorded lyre. The lyre's body is made of a tortoise-shell. The black bird in front of the head presents a problem. Its colour suggests it is a crow and it could symbolise Coronis, the beautiful daughter of the king Phlegyas, whom Apollo loved.

The Room of the Showcases (13)

The last room before the exit contains exhibits of all different periods and different kinds of art. Moving anti-clockwise from the exit staircase:

Case 1. Top and bottom shelves: Mycenaean clay vases (1400-1100 BC) from the cemeteries at Delphi.

Middle shelf: Mycenaean clay figurines from the Apollo Sanctuary (**3286, 2647**) and from the Pronaia Sanctuary. On the left is a portrait head of an unknown man (**1706**) supposed to be the Roman consul, Titus Quintius Flamininus, the conqueror of Philip V of Macedon at the Battle of Cynoscephalae (197 BC). A beautiful early 2nd century BC piece.

Case 2. Finds from excavations at Krisa and Kirrha, the port of Delphi (a trip to the coast, east of Itea to Galaxidi and west to Kirrha, Antikirrha and Medeon is rewarding). They date from Early Helladic to Late Helladic (Mycenaean) times, about 2800-1200 BC.

There follows a herm (**4070**) which carried the protome of Plutarch, the well-known philosopher and biographer (46-120 AD), who was a priest of Apollo for many years. The inscription relates that the protome was an offering from his compatriots at Chaeronea and Delphi.

Next is a beautiful marble statue of a kore dressed in a thick chiton (**1791** and **3333**). It is similar to the monuments of korai in the temples of Artemis Brauroneia and Eileithya. Early 3rd century BC.

On the other side of the entrance is the marble statue of a child holding a goose (**4755**) also an offering to Apollo. Late 3rd century BC.

The Parian marble statue portrays Antinous, a youth from Bithynia in Asia Minor, famous for his beauty and the favourite of the Emperor Hadrian. He was drowned while accompanying Hadrian up the Nile in 130 AD. Legends grew up around his death, one of which was that he gave his life for the emperor. Hadrian had him deified in many places and built Antinoupolis in Egypt. Elsewhere Antinous was honoured by festivals, statues, etc. At Delphi he is portrayed as a god, perhaps wearing a golden crown, as holes in his hair band indicate. His white, smooth and shining body contrasts to the different colour of his curly hair. The black marble base also emphasises the whiteness of the body. There are many cult statues of Antinous in existence, but that at Delphi is one of the better ones. It illustrates the 2nd century AD revival of romanticism, which found expression in religion and the arts, using ancient Greek prototypes. The craftsman who made this statue must have been one of the better ones of the decade of 130 AD.

The portrait protome (**5667**) next to Antinous is in contrast to the spirit of the statue. It belongs to a herm and portrays an unknown philosopher of imperial times. It is a good example of the 2nd century AD art of portraiture. The philosopher is now introverted. His was a world which was slowly dying, as it was not renewed by new, vital ideas, and finally the spread of christianity put an end to it.

In the last case finds from the Corycian Cave, a sacred cave on Parnassos, are displayed. The higher peaks of Parnassos, Liakoura and Gerontobrachos, rise to 2459 m and 2435 m respectively and the Corycian Cave is 1360 m up. It is now accessible by car from Arachova and has wonderful views from different places around (Palaiopanayia, Kroki, Kalania) of the peaks and wooded mountainsides.

There is a magnificent view from the brow of the mountain where the traditional road ascended to the Cave: Delphi and the plain of Amphissa, the mountains of Central Greece, Kirphys and Helicon, the Corinthian Gulf and the mountains of the Peloponnese beyond can all be made out. The Cave lies near the acropolis of the prehistoric site of Lycoreia, which can be seen from its entrance. Excavations have taken place in the entrance and interior of the cave (maximum width about 60 m and length about 90 m), which contains stalagmites and stalactites and inscriptions cut in the rock.

Case 3. Top shelf: a clay plaque with a black figure scene on a white ground of Apollo and Heracles wrestling for the Delphic tripod (see also Room 3, the pediment of the Siphnian Treasury); a small bronze Geometric horse; clay figurines, etc.

Middle shelf: a unique terracotta votive group of the Nine Muses listening to Pan playing his pipe; clay and bronze figurines of piglets, tortoises, birds and seated female figures; bone combs, a flute, etc.

Bottom shelf: a terracotta plaque with a black figure scene of Satyrs.

1. *Marble statuette of a girl.*
2. *Portrait of a philosopher.*

Marble statue of Antinoos.

Detail of the statue of Antinoos.▶

Portrait, probably of T. Q. Flamininus.

Outside the Museum. The typical Early Christian mosaic floor comes from a 5th century AD basilica found in 1959 in present village of Delphi. Human figures, animals, fish and plants are depicted in a variety of colours. The Roman marble sarcophagus was found in the east cemetery. It shows the Calydonian boar and two griffins each side of a torch. The dead man is shown reclining on the lid.

In front of the Office are some very interesting sculptures and architectural fragments. The relief base of the monument of Aemilius Paulus is among them (site plan no. 53) and the central figure of Apollo from the east pediment of the temple, which recently has been identified.

In the covered area, a part from the architectural fragments, a female statue and other finds, some of the numerous inscriptions are accessible. Most are from offerings. They bring to mind the fact that Delphi does not only furnish marvellous examples of craftsmanship, but also much information about life in the ancient world.